THE BOOK OF
CROSS-STITCH

THE BOOK OF
CROSS-STITCH

Traditional and Contemporary Designs
for Holidays and Special Occasions

GAIL LAWTHER

Watson-Guptill Publications/New York

Published in 1994 in the United States
by Watson-Guptill Publications,
a division of BPI Communications, Inc.,
1515 Broadway, New York, N.Y. 10036

Cataloging in Publication Data is available
from the Library of Congress.

ISBN 0-8230-0517-8

Manufactured in Singapore

First printing, 1994

1 2 3 4 5 6 7 8 9 / 02 01 00 99 98 97 96 95 94

■
ACKNOWLEDGEMENTS
■

Thanks very much to the following people for their
stitching skills:

Liz Lance: nativity picture (page 90)
Christopher Lawther: holly wreath (page 96)
Rachel McIntyre: photograph frame (page 32),
    Easter egg-cosy (page 84) and angel table-mat
    (page 102)
Jennie Ring: bluebird picture (page 36)
Sue Slide: wedding sampler (page 28), nursery
    sampler (page 62), Easter-egg picture (page 80)
    and angel table-mat (page 102)
Ally Smith: anniversary sampler (page 48), baby
    blanket (page 66) and Chinese-style initial
    (page 110)

All designs are by Gail Lawther

CONTENTS

INTRODUCTION 6

CROSS-STITCH TIPS 8

BIRTHDAYS 12
BIRTHDAY CARD 14
BIRTHDAY PLAQUE 18
CAKE RIBBON 22

WEDDINGS 26
WEDDING SAMPLER 28
PHOTOGRAPH FRAME 32
BLUEBIRD PICTURE 36

ANNIVERSARIES 42
HEART PICTURE 44
ANNIVERSARY SAMPLER 48
CELTIC LOVE-KNOT PICTURE 52

BIRTHS 56
INITIAL CARD 58
NURSERY SAMPLER 62
BABY BLANKET 66

EASTER 72
SPRING-FLOWERS PICTURE 74
EASTER-EGG PICTURE 80
EASTER EGG-COSY 84

CHRISTMAS 88
NATIVITY PICTURE 90
HOLLY WREATH 96
ANGEL TABLE-MAT 102

OTHER SPECIAL OCCASIONS 108
CHINESE-STYLE INITIAL 110
MULTI-COLOURED ALPHABET 116

CHARTS FOR YOUR OWN DESIGNS 122

MANUFACTURERS AND SUPPLIERS 128

INTRODUCTION

Special occasions call for special things to remember them by, and that is what this book is all about. Many of us are disillusioned with over-priced, mass-produced presents and cards, and want to give the people we care for something more personal and memorable.

In the pages of this book you will find ideas for birthdays, weddings, anniversaries, Christmas and Easter, plus items which you can make for a new baby, and several projects that you can adapt to suit virtually any occasion. Each project has full instructions and materials lists for working it, and suggestions for alternative ways of stitching the project to make it unique to you.

Cross stitch is a surprisingly versatile form of needlecraft, and I have taken the inspiration for these designs from many different sources, ranging from South American crib scenes to Victorian filet lace. You will find traditional and modern ideas, pastel and bold colour schemes, detailed and naïve designs, large and small projects. Each project has been marked with an 'easiness' rating and a 'time-to-stitch' rating, as these are not necessarily the same; within each project you will also find a box of tips, which will provide specialist help for stitching that particular item.

Many of the projects can be personalized in different ways, and in the relevant sections you will find suggestions and charts for alternative letters or numbers. Finally, at the back of the book you will find more pages of chart patterns – borders, motifs and repeat patterns – which you can add to the projects within the book or use to build up your own designs and colour schemes.

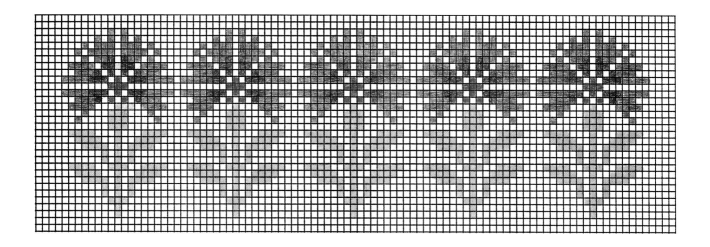

Opposite: Multi-coloured alphabet. Cross stitch is simple to learn and beautiful results can be achieved quickly and easily. This colourful alphabet would make good present for a friend or relative when a more traditional or seasonal gift would not be suitable. The project can be found on page 116.

CROSS-STITCH TIPS

If you have never done any cross stitch before, rest assured: it couldn't be easier. Almost all the charts in the book are worked in exactly the same way, using exactly the same stitch, with the occasional addition of some backstitch on outlines. This section will introduce you to the basic principles of working with cross stitch, with hints on how to make the final pressing and mounting of your work as easy as possible.

■

CROSS STITCH

■

The basic cross stitch consists of one diagonal stitch crossed over by another to form a cross filling a square shape (a). As each cross fills a square so neatly, cross-stitch charts are drawn in squares (b); each square (unless otherwise indicated) represents one cross stitch.

Generally, you will find yourself working rows of cross stitch rather than isolated stitches here and there. Whenever you have a line of squares in one colour, showing that a row of cross stitches is all to be worked in the same colour, you can work the stitches in one block. It is possible to work both stitches of each individual cross before moving on to the next, but it is much quicker, and also much neater, if you work all the underneath diagonal stitches in a block first (c), and then go back and cross them with the top diagonal stitches (d). I find it easiest to work blocks of stitches from the top downward first, forming a row of single diagonals, and then to go back up the row working the top stitches. In this way, I can keep the needle in a horizontal position all the time and take it in and out of the fabric in one movement.

As I am right-handed, I also work across the canvas or background fabric from right to left, working each new block to the left of the old one (e). This means that when I am putting the needle downward into the canvas I am going into a so-called 'dirty' hole – one that has a stitch already in

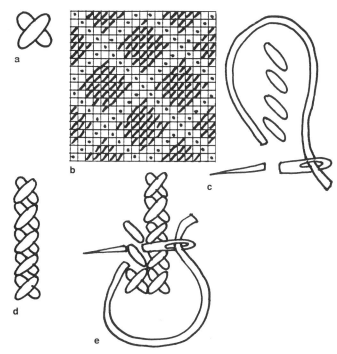

it – and coming up into a 'clean' hole, making it less likely that I will bring unwanted threads or fibres to the surface. If you are left-handed, you should reverse this way of working.

You may like to stretch your canvas very tightly to stop it from puckering. If you do so, you will find it harder to take your needle in and out of the fabric in one movement, and you may need to use the tapestry or quilting method of working, with one hand underneath the frame to guide the needle to the surface, and one hand at the top of the work to guide it back down the new hole. If you do work in this way, you may prefer to work rows of stitches from side to side instead of up and down.

When you are starting off threads, don't use a knot. Knots can come undone, and they will also spoil the flat appearance of your work when you mount it. Instead, pull your needle through so that there is about half an inch of thread left behind the canvas, then hold this in position while you work your next few stitches. As you take the first stitches of the row, catch the loose thread down on the back with them (f). This method is much more secure and lies flatter.

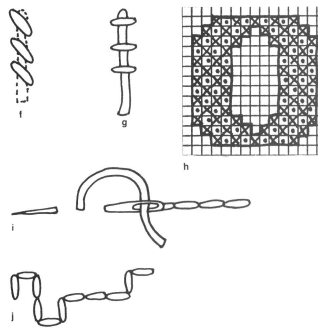

Backstitch is worked in a straight line by bringing the needle up one square ahead of the last stitch; you then take the needle down into the end of the last stitch and bring it up one square further ahead on the stitching line, in one movement (**i**). If you are working backstitch round an uneven shape, you use the same principle but follow the stitching line as it meanders (**j**).

Start and finish off backstitch threads by running them under a few stitches at the back of the canvas.

MATERIALS

Most cross stitch is worked on some kind of even-weave fabric, so that you can easily see where the stitches should go and can count blocks of stitches accurately. The most common background fabric is Aida, which is woven so that it produces a square pattern with large holes at the corners. Aida is available in a wide range of different colours, and also in many different gauges; it is usually described as so many holes per inch, generally abbreviated to *hpi*. The greater the number of holes per inch, the more cross stitches will fit into a smaller area, and the smaller your design will be. If you wish to enlarge or reduce a pattern, simply stitch it on Aida of fewer or more holes per inch. Aida-type fabrics with very few holes per inch (e.g., 6–8) are often known as Binca. Hardanger is a fine fabric, similar to Aida and available in the smaller gauges.

Cross stitch can also be carried out on many other kinds of evenweave backgrounds. Linen and linen-mix fabrics are very popular; with these, you may have to work each stitch over three, four or five threads in order to form a cross of a reasonable size. Ordinary needlepoint canvas can easily be used for cross stitch, but is best for designs in which you won't be leaving any areas blank, as it is transparent. Plastic canvas pieces are regular grids of plastic which can be used for large-scale cross stitch; they are available in squares and rectangles, as well as in circles, diamonds and other shapes.

If you wish to work any of the designs in this book – or any other cross-stitch designs – on to a fabric without an even weave, this is still possible using a method called *waste canvas*. Tack a piece of special canvas on to your area to be stitched, then work the design over the grid so that your needle also goes through your underneath fabric (the waste canvas

Similarly, when you are finishing off threads, do so by running the needle under a few neighbouring stitches before you cut the end (**g**). Don't take threads from one area of a design to another behind the fabric unless you can be quite sure that they won't show on the surface; it is much better to finish off each section of the design neatly and then start afresh on the next part with a new thread.

One thing is very important when you are working cross stitch: every top diagonal stitch on your project should lie in the same direction. This gives a neat appearance and texture to the finished work. If you always keep your work with the same part at the top, and work across the rows in a logical way, this will happen automatically, but there are bound to be times when you wish to turn the canvas round. If so, make sure that you turn it 180°; then you can carry on as normal and your stitches will still lie in the same direction.

BACKSTITCH

Backstitch is sometimes used to highlight outlines and to separate blocks of similar-coloured cross stitch. When you see a solid line around the edge of a square on a chart (**h**), this indicates that the line should be worked in backstitch. Unless stated otherwise, it is usually worked in one strand of cotton and across one square of the canvas.

gives you the regular grid so that you can count the stitches as usual). When the design is complete, dampen the canvas with water to dissolve the glue that has been holding the threads stable, and pull the canvas threads out one by one, leaving the cross-stitch design on your background fabric.

THREADS

Virtually any thread can be used for cross stitch, although some are more successful than others. The most popular threads are stranded cottons (which come twisted in strands of six threads and can be subdivided); *coton perle* (which has a tight twist and an attractive sheen); tapestry wool (a matt, loosely woven wool); and soft cotton (a thick, matt thread). Metallic threads of different kinds and thicknesses are also used for highlights and special effects, as are opalescent, shiny viscose and fluorescent threads. The metallic threads which contain some cotton as well as metal or lurex are often the easiest to use, but manufacturers are bringing out specialist threads that are more and more easy to manage.

When you are cutting your threads, don't use pieces that are too long. If you do, they will get worn through by being taken down and up through the canvas over and over again and are likely to break or buckle, wasting thread and spoiling the appearance of your work. If your length of thread starts to fray, finish it off and start afresh. If you are using stranded cotton, soft cotton or *coton perle*, an occasional twist of the needle in the direction of the twist of the thread will keep your thread looking its best.

NEEDLES

If you are using a background fabric which already has holes in it, as you will be doing for most of the projects in this book, you will find it easiest to use a tapestry needle rather than a conventional needle. Tapestry needles have blunt tips so that they go neatly through the holes in the fabric without splitting the threads, and are available in many sizes. Different people prefer different combinations (e.g., a fine needle body with a long eye, or a medium needle body with a medium eye), so in each project I have just given recommendations for fine, medium or large tapestry needles, which refers to the thickness of the body of the needle.

WORKING WITH CHARTS

Some of the charts in the book are in colour and others are in black and white. Colour charts are generally used where there are many different colours of threads in the finished design, as the coloured areas make it easier to see where you are on the chart. On coloured charts you will find matching coloured blocks in a key, and beside each coloured block a number will tell you the number of the thread used for all the blocks in that colour. Black-and-white charts are used where there is only one colour of thread (e.g., the Angel table-mat on page 103), or where there are only a few. If there is more than one colour, each will have a different symbol, for instance a dot or a diagonal line. Once again, a key will show you each symbol, and alongside each symbol is the number of the thread used to stitch each square marked in that way. With either colour or black-and-white charts you may find it helpful to have a photocopy made of the one you are working on; you can then carry it around with you more easily, and it will be easier to turn round to suit the area you are working.

On some of the charts you will find arrows at one side and at the top or bottom. These mark the central lines of the design horizontally and vertically. In most projects you will be instructed to mark the central lines of your piece of fabric with tacking threads, or with a fading pen (the marks fade within about twenty-four hours). When you begin stitching, you will generally start (unless specified otherwise in the instructions) at the centre of the fabric, where your two lines meet; this corresponds to the centre of your chart, where the horizontal and vertical lines meet. Generally you will work outward from the centre of the chart, counting rows and stitches as you go to make sure that you are stitching exactly the pattern that is shown on the chart. If you are working from a photocopy, you may find it helpful to cross off each line of stitching as you work it, and you can then see exactly which row you have to stitch next.

When you are stitching a design which has lots of different colours next to each other in the same row of the chart (such as the Spring-flowers picture on page 75) it is best to work each block of stitching that requires the same colour rather than working all the way up and down one row before starting the next. So, for instance, on that picture you would work all the pale yellow on one petal of a daffodil before changing threads and working the darker yellow shading within it.

PRESSING YOUR WORK

If you press embroidery on the front it flattens the stitches and spoils the effect, so you need to press it from behind. Lay the embroidery face-down on a soft cloth to protect the stitching, and press on the reverse with a warm steam iron. If the grain of the fabric becomes misaligned during stitching, pull the grain straight by pulling the corners of the embroidery outward, and then iron into place.

If you are going to be stitching a seam using your cross-stitch embroidery – for instance, if you are making a design into a pincushion or a cushion cover – it can be helpful to attach a layer of Vilene or similar iron-on fusible fabric at this stage, before you cut the design down to size. Cross-stitch fabrics are usually quite loosely woven, and the Vilene holds the strands in place and helps to stop them fraying.

STRETCHING YOUR WORK

Cross-stitch projects look best if they are well-stretched over a flat background. This can be done by folding the edges over a stiff board and lacing them together to provide the tension, but a better – and easier and quicker – method is to use adhesive cardboard or mounting board. This is sold in some needlework shops and in specialist craft shops, and is also found in some needlework frame kits. When you have trimmed your needlework to size and pressed it, peel off the protective layer from the card to expose a sticky surface. Lay your embroidery face-up on this, adjust the position, and then press it firmly into place. If you have a frame which covers the edges of the backing card, you don't need to turn the edges of the fabric over to the back of the card – just trim them to the same size.

FRAMING YOUR WORK

Some cross-stitch projects lend themselves very well to being stretched over embroidery hoops as frames. Specialized hoops are also available, where the embroidery is stretched between an outer and an inner frame. Small projects look good mounted as cards. You can now buy card 'blanks' with virtually any shaped aperture: not just square, rectangular, circular or oval, but arched, shaped like birds, flowers or bells, or with several apertures.

For a semi-permanent frame, mounting board can be used; this is available in a wide range of colours, and occasionally in attractive textures and finishes such as linen-weave or marbled.

If you want a really durable frame for your work, you will need to buy a frame kit or have a suitable frame made. Frame kits are now also available in many different shapes and sizes, including arches, circles and ovals, and more bizarre shapes such as apples and bells, as well as conventional rectangles and the harder-to-find squares. Try your embroidery in your chosen frame to see whether you wish to mount it plain, or whether you want one or more coloured mounts around it. Many embroideries look best without glass, and can be coated thinly with a tapestry spray for protection.

BIRTHDAYS

BIRTHDAY CARD

Easiness rating: easy
Time-to-stitch rating: fairly quick

This pretty rainbow design is suitable for any birthday, and for anyone from a child to a pensioner. The shapes are easy to stitch, and the clouds are given an extra glisten from a strand of opalescent thread which is mixed in with the white during stitching. I have listed the numbers for the threads in the rainbow colours, but don't feel that you have to follow them exactly; this is an ideal project for using up scraps of threads, as long as the colours go well together. As a variation you could stitch the rainbow in pastel shades instead, on a background of white with a hint of blue.

MATERIALS

- One piece of white or pale blue Aida, 20 × 15 cm (8 × 6 in), 12 hpi
- Anchor stranded cotton, one skein each (unless specified otherwise) in the following colours:
  - 001 white
  - 094 purple
  - 132 blue
  - 245 green
  - 290 yellow
  - 316 orange
  - 046 red
  - 144 pale blue (two skeins)
- Opalescent thread, such as Kreinik blending filament 032, Madeira Metallic No. 120 shade 310, or Madeira Metallic No. 40 shade 380
- Medium tapestry needle
- Blue card blank with a rectangular aperture 9 × 12·5 cm (3½ × 5½ in)
- Craft glue

PREPARATION

1 Press the piece of Aida and check it to make sure that the grain is straight; if not, pull it into shape as you press.

2 Mark the centre of your piece of Aida with lines of tacking or with a fading pen.

STITCHING

3 Using three strands of cotton in your needle, follow the chart overleaf and stitch the rainbow, beginning from the centre point marked and working outward.
4 Using two strands of white cotton and one strand of opalescent thread in your needle, stitch the clouds, following the chart.
5 Using three strands of cotton, stitch the pale blue background; you will find it easy to fill these areas in as the straight edges of the clouds act as markers for the edges of the design.

FINISHING

6 Remove the marking threads, if used.
7 Lay the embroidery face-down on a soft cloth and press on the reverse side with a warm steam iron, straightening the grain if necessary.
8 Trim the edges of the Aida so that the fabric is slightly smaller than the size of the card blank.
9 Open up the card blank and lay it face-down on a flat surface. Spread a thin layer of glue around the inside of the central panel.
10 Position the embroidery, face-down, on to the central panel so that the design is centred in the aperture. Make sure that the design is the right way up when you look at the card! Press the edges of the fabric down on to the glue so that the design is taut and the edges are well-secured.
11 With the card blank still face-down, spread a thin layer of glue over the inside of the left-hand panel. Fold the glued side over the back of the embroidery and press firmly into position.
12 Leave the card to dry under a flat weight, such as a heavy book.

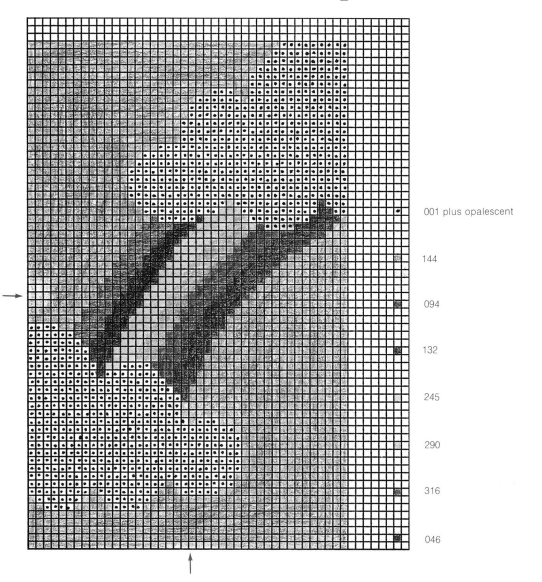

001 plus opalescent

144

094

132

245

290

316

046

TIPS

● Opalescent threads are generally slightly more difficult to handle than ordinary cotton; they tend to tangle, and may wear through more easily. Keep problems to a minimum by using short lengths of thread when you are stitching the cloud.

● When you are mounting the card, make sure that you only apply a thin layer of glue; if you use too much, the card mount will buckle and you will spoil its appearance.

● If you can't find a card blank of the colour that you want, make your own out of thin card. Cut a rectangle the same height as you want the finished card and three times the width, and fold each side inward. Cut an aperture of the right size in the middle section for mounting the embroidery.

■

VARIATION

■

Stitching the rainbow card is fairly time-consuming, and you will probably only want to stitch it for a really special birthday. If you are looking for a quick idea that can be rustled up in only a few minutes, try this cheerful balloon design. It was stitched in three strands of jade cotton on a pale green Aida background. The string was added in a single thread of black backstitch, and a ready-made pale aquamarine bow was stitched in the position marked by the solid block on the chart. Finally, the design was finished off and mounted in the same way as the large card.

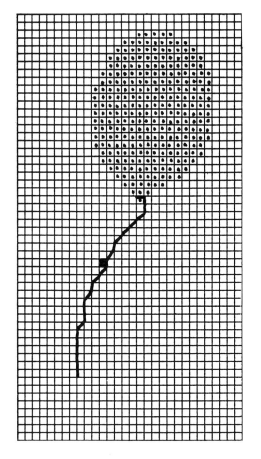

BIRTHDAY PLAQUE

Easiness rating: very easy
Time-to-stitch rating: very quick

When a really significant birthday comes around, such as an eighteenth, twenty-first or fiftieth, it is a good opportunity to make a card-cum-present that is a little bit different. This birthday plaque has been stitched to celebrate an eighteenth birthday, but the same idea can be adapted to any number using the charts overleaf. Of course, you don't have to confine it to birthdays; this design lends itself well to anniversary celebrations as well.

The plaque has been stitched using one of the squares of silky damask produced especially for cross-stitch embroidery, which are available in several colours and many designs. This project requires one of the circular designs that has a central circle of 39 × 39 holes across the diameter. For a different look, you could stitch the numbers in a different colour, picking up the new colour in the card mount, or on a cream or pastel background instead of white.

Using the charts and your chosen colours you can create a present that will be treasured forever.

■ MATERIALS ■

- One white damask cross-stitch panel, with a central circle 39 holes in diameter
- Anchor stranded cotton, one skein each in the following colours:
    - 108 mauve
    - 112 purple
- Gutermann metallic thread, one spool of 041 silver
- Medium tapestry needle
- Purple mounting card, 30 cm (12 in) square, with a circle 23 cm (9 in) in diameter cut from the centre
- Craft glue
- White backing card, 30 cm (12 in) square

■ PREPARATION ■

1 Lay the damask square face-down and press it gently on the reverse side with a warm steam iron.
2 Mark the centre of the circle with tacking threads.

■ STITCHING ■

3 Using three strands of mauve cotton in your needle, stitch your chosen numbers by following the chart overleaf. Start each number three squares out from the central line that you have tacked from top to bottom of the circle, and make sure that the halfway points on the numbers, marked on the chart, align with the line that you have tacked from side to side of the circle.
4 Using one strand of purple cotton in your needle, outline the numbers in backstitch.
5 Using one strand of silver thread, work backstitch around the margin of the central circle on the damask to form a simple edging.

■ FINISHING ■

6 Remove the tacking threads. Lay the embroidery face-down on a soft cloth and press gently on the reverse side with a warm steam iron. Straighten the grain of the fabric if necessary as you press.
7 Trim the square of damask down so that it is just under 30 cm (12 in) square.
8 Lay the purple mount on top of the square of backing card so that the edges align, and use a pencil to draw the position of the round aperture on to the backing card.
9 Put the purple mount face-down and spread the back with a thin layer of glue.
10 Position the embroidery face-down so that the

design is centred in the circular aperture. Press the fabric down on to the glue so that the embroidery is stretched taut and is well-secured.

11 Place the backing card marked-side up, and spread a fairly thick layer of glue around the edges, outside the marked circle. Do not spread glue *inside* the circle, as it could come through the fabric and spoil it.

12 Position the purple mount, face-up, on top of the backing card so that the edges align. Press firmly to make the glue adhere.

13 Press overnight under a flat weight such as a heavy book.

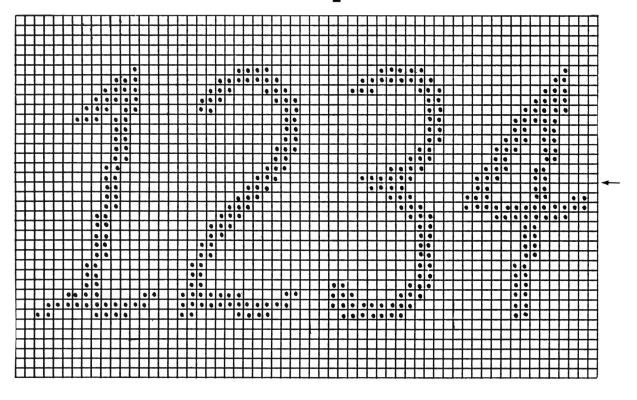

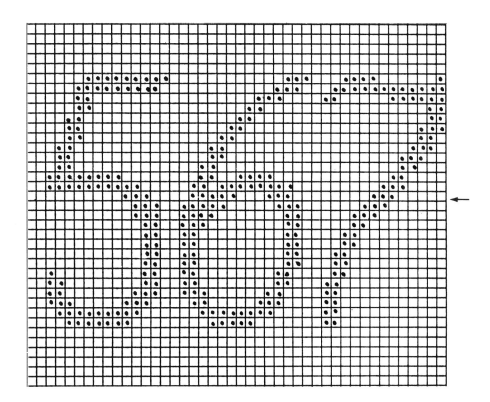

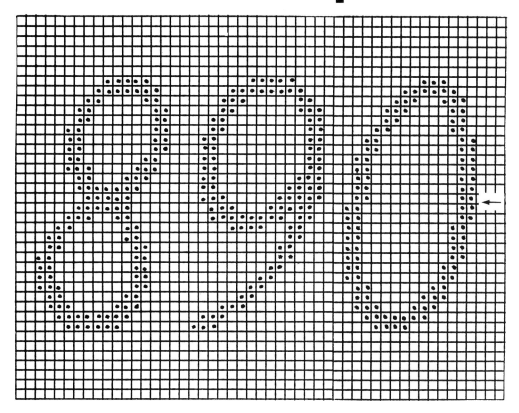

TIPS

● As with the opalescent thread in the previous project, metallic thread can be harder to work with than ordinary cottons. Keep problems to a minimum by only using short lengths of thread in your needle.

● The squares of damask panels tend to be woven fairly loosely, so make sure that you don't pull your stitching too tight and make them gape. Pull each stitch through firmly but gently until it is lying flat.

● When you are counting your three squares out from the central line so that you know where to start each number, make sure that you are counting to the outermost square of each number, not necessarily to the square at which you will start stitching.

■

VARIATIONS

■

Use the numbers on the charts to make your own multiple figures for special birthdays or anniversaries. If you wish to stitch something special for a silver, ruby, golden or pearl wedding anniversary, choose appropriate colours for the embroidery threads and the mounts – you could even add beads that pick up the theme, or incorporate fake jewels into the design.

You can also make these damask squares into cushions – in fact, some of them are sold ready-made as cushion-covers. To adapt your square, stitch it to a matching backing square, perhaps adding a ruffle of lace or *broderie anglaise*, and stuff it gently with wadding, stuffing, herbs or *pot pourri* before completing the seam on the final side.

CAKE RIBBON

Easiness rating: very easy
Time-to-stitch rating: very quick

It is always nice to personalize a cake, and if your icing skills aren't up to the task, how about using your stitching talents instead? The ribbon shown opposite can be adapted to go around virtually any cake; simply buy a piece of tape a little longer than the cake's circumference. Stitch the name, and, if you wish, add some simple candles (if the number of the birthday isn't too daunting, you could even add the right number of candles!).

The tape that I have used for the ribbon is cross-stitch tape, which is made in a 5 cm (2 in) width with 27 holes across. This piece has silver edging, but it is also available in gold, and in a range of pastel and bright colours; you can also buy the same tape in cream rather than white, so choose the colour scheme that suits your cake best. To pick up the glitter of the edging I have used one thread of stranded cotton and one thread of a matching metallic; you could choose a metallic thread that ties in with your colour scheme, or stitch the name just in stranded cotton.

■

MATERIALS

■

- One piece of cross-stitch tape, 5 cm (2 in) longer than the circumference of your cake
- One skein of stranded cotton in your chosen colour (I have used Anchor 189)
- One spool of metallic thread in your chosen colour (I have used Gutermann 235)
- Scraps of stranded cotton in pastel colours, including yellow for the flames
- Fine tapestry needle

■

PREPARATION

■

1 Press the piece of cross-stitch tape. Check to make sure that it is straight; if not, pull the grain into shape as you press. Fold the tape gently in half to mark the halfway point.

2 On a piece of graph paper, use the chart on pages 24 and 25 to plot the name that you wish to stitch. Position the letters so that they look right (this may mean that you have uneven spaces between them).

3 Once you are happy with the chart you have plotted, mark the central point along the top and bottom.

■

STITCHING

■

4 Using one strand of stranded cotton and one strand of metallic thread in your needle, begin at the centre of the ribbon and work from the centre of your chart outward. All the letters begin on the fifth square in from the top and bottom of the tape.

5 Once the name is complete, use the candle chart to stitch a group of candles on each side of the name, starting ten squares away from the beginning and end of the name.

I have reversed the chart for the right-hand side of the ribbon so that the groups of candles are symmetrical. Use two strands of stranded cotton, using a random pattern of pastel colours for the candles and yellow for the flames.

■

FINISHING

■

6 Lay the tape face-down on a soft cloth and press it gently on the reverse side with a warm steam iron.

7 Position the tape round your cake, fold in the raw edges of the tape at the back, and pin to the cake. Cover the join with a flower or bow if you wish.

TIPS

● As always with metallic threads, use just a short length in your needle so that it doesn't tangle.

● If you use a darker-coloured background tape for your cake ribbon, you may wish to use brighter colours for your candles so that they stand out well — or you could do them all in the same colour if you choose a strong one.

● The tape tends to be fairly translucent, so if you are using a strong-coloured thread, don't take it from one letter to another behind the stitching; finish each letter off separately.

VARIATIONS

You don't need to confine yourself to birthdays with this cake ribbon; it is ideal for a special occasion such as an anniversary or wedding as well. In this case, work out two names on your chart, perhaps adding some extra symbols such as flowers, hearts or bluebirds taken from the wedding and anniversary sections of the book. Then simply find the central point, as before, and stitch in the usual way. You could also use it as an extra-special ribbon around a birthday or wedding present.

This letterform is attractive and has many other uses as well as the cake ribbon. Try stitching a single initial on to a card or plaque; use it to stitch whole names for a wedding or anniversary card; or combine it with some of the motifs in the final section (see pages 123–7) as a sampler. For an older person's special birthday, perhaps a seventieth, eightieth or ninetieth, you could stitch in the right number of candles in rows above and below the name!

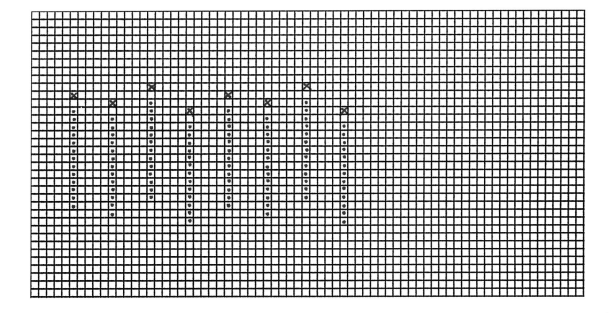

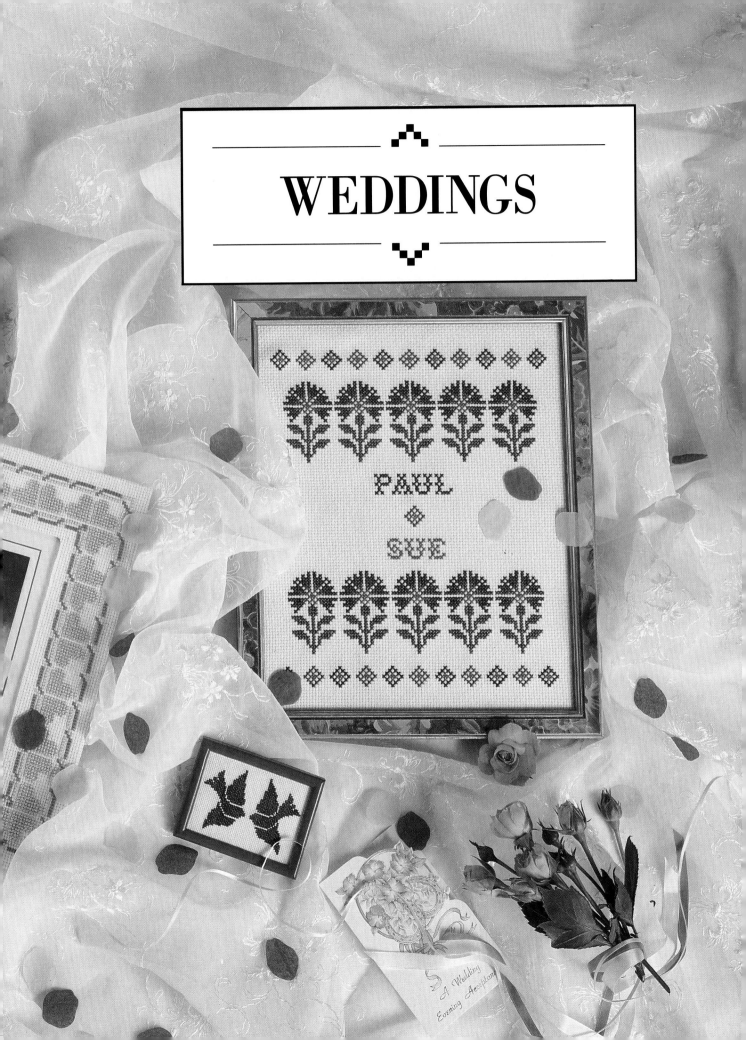

WEDDINGS

WEDDING SAMPLER

Easiness rating: fairly easy
Time-to-stitch rating: quick to medium

All couples like to have a permanent reminder of their wedding day, and if it is one that has been designed and stitched for them, it will be even more special. This pretty sampler uses a modern version of a traditional carnation motif – the carnation is a pattern that has appeared on samplers for several centuries in different forms. The cream background and rich colours complement the formal design. For the names, use the alphabet on pages 50–1; if you wish to add a date as well, make an extra line on the chart or put it in instead of the central diamond. When it comes to choosing your frame, pick one, if you can, that reflects some of the bright colours of the flowers.

■

MATERIALS

■

- One piece of cream Aida, 36 × 31 cm (14 × 12 in), 11 hpi
- DMC stranded cotton, one skein each in the following colours:
    - 602 pink
    - 796 blue
    - 333 purple
    - 991 green
- A frame of your choice to fit the finished sampler

■

PREPARATION

■

1 Press the piece of Aida.
2 Use tacking threads or a fading pen to mark the central point of your fabric.

3 On graph paper, chart the names that you wish to use, following the alphabet on pages 50–1. If you would like to put in a date as well, use the chart of numerals overleaf.
4 Mark the centre point of each name, and of the date if you are using one.

■

STITCHING

■

5 Using three strands of cotton, begin stitching the central diamond. (If you are using a date instead of the central diamond, stitch it in your chosen colour so that it is centred around the vertical line marking the centre of the fabric.)
6 Add the names on the lines shown on the chart, starting in the centre and working outward in the colour indicated.
7 Stitch the rest of the design by following the chart, working outward from the names. When you come to stitch the diamonds at the top and bottom, check that they line up with the flowers and leaves as they should so that the design is symmetrical.

■

FINISHING

■

8 Remove any tacking threads. Lay the embroidery face-down on a soft cloth and press it gently on the reverse side with a warm steam iron. Straighten the grain of the fabric if necessary while you press it.
9 Fit the embroidery into your chosen frame, trimming and stretching the fabric and adding mounts as required.

602

796

333

991

● Make sure that you finish each thread off neatly in the stitching; don't take threads across from one flower to another, as the colours are fairly dark and will show through the backing fabric.

● If you would like a softer look for your finished sampler, stitch it in pastel shades of mauve, baby blue, pale pink and pale green, perhaps on a white background so that the colours show up well.

VARIATION

Scraps of thread and Aida left over from the main sampler were used to stitch this delicate little picture, which simply uses two of the carnations from the chart. The picture looks quite dramatic mounted in a silk frame that picks up the pink in the centres of the flowers. A single flower could be used as a central motif on a greetings card.

PHOTOGRAPH FRAME

Easiness rating: medium
Time-to-stitch rating: medium

If you are looking for a unique wedding present to make for a couple, this photograph frame could be just the answer. It is stitched in a simple pattern of pink hearts with a double border of pink-and-yellow intertwining lines, and is worked on a cream background for a soft effect; the *coton perle* threads give a gentle sheen to the stitching. The colour scheme shown here would be ideal for a wedding photograph featuring a dress and flowers in cream or ivory, but if the colour scheme of your couple's wedding was different, you could always alter your colour scheme accordingly – for instance, you might like to pick up the colours in the bride's bouquet, or the colour of the groom's buttonhole or tie!

Don't be daunted by mounting the frame; it is easily done using a shape cut from cardboard or from sticky board such as Pres-On. With sticky board, one side is coated with adhesive and protected by a layer of plastic, and when you are ready to mount the embroidery you simply peel off the protective layer and press the back of the embroidery on to the board, which both stretches and secures it at the same time.

■
MATERIALS
■

- One piece of cream Aida, 41 × 36 cm (16 × 14 in), 12 hpi
- DMC *coton perle* in the following colours:
    - 776 light pink (two skeins)
    - 956 dark pink (one skein)
    - 743 yellow (one skein)
- One piece of sticky board (e.g., Pres-On), 31 × 26 cm (12¼ × 10¼ in)
- Medium or large tapestry needle
- Craft glue or a hot-glue gun
- Craft knife
- Masking tape

■
PREPARATION
■

1 Press the piece of Aida fabric, straightening the grain if necessary.
2 At one corner of the piece of Aida, measure in 3·5 cm (1½ in) from the top and the side, and mark the corresponding square. As this design has no centre, this is where you will begin your embroidery.

■
STITCHING
■

3 Beginning on the marked square and at one corner of the chart overleaf, use one thickness of *coton perle* in each colour to stitch the design, following the chart. Stitch a small section of the border first, then stitch all the pink hearts (doing these first will make it easier to see if you go wrong). You can then finish off the inside and outside borders.

■
FINISHING
■

4 Lay the embroidery face-down on a soft cloth and press on the reverse side using a warm steam iron; straighten the grain of the fabric if necessary while you are pressing.
5 On the piece of adhesive cardboard, measure and mark a border 6·5 cm (2½ in) all the way round.
6 Using a craft knife, cut away the central rectangle of the cardboard to leave the shape of the frame.
7 Peel off the protective backing from the cardboard to expose the adhesive.
8 Position the embroidery carefully over the frame so that the design is placed exactly in the centre of

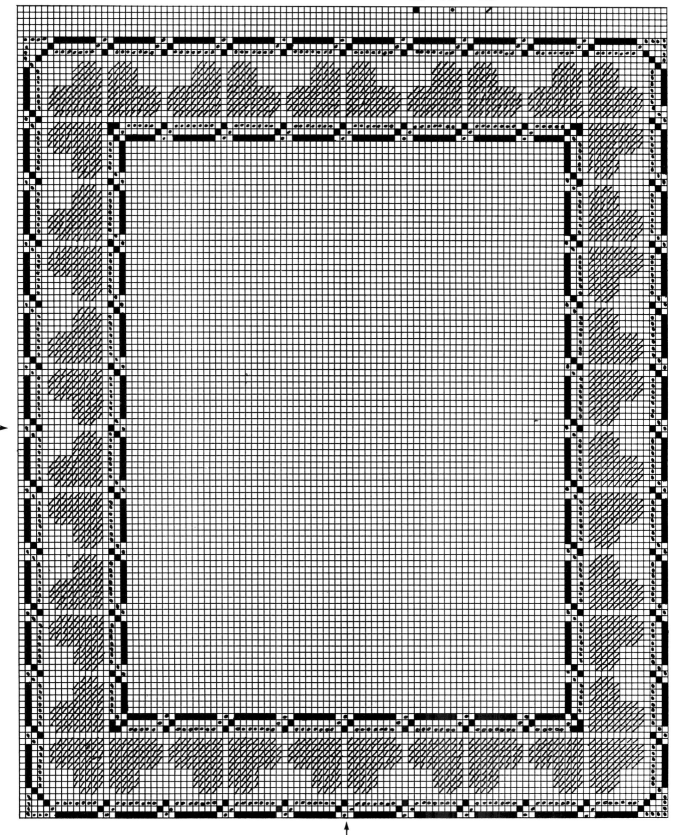

34

each edge of the frame. When you are happy with the positioning, press the embroidery down firmly so that it is secured against the adhesive.

9 Trim the fabric around the outside of the frame and around the inside edge so that it is 2·5 cm (1 in) larger than the cardboard all round.

10 Turn the raw edges of the fabric over to the back, clipping the corners on the inside, and stick into place with craft glue or a hot-glue gun.

11 Cover the raw edges with masking tape to neaten them.

12 Your frame is now ready for a photograph; slip a photo behind it, then seal the back with a piece of cardboard or paper just slightly smaller than the frame itself.

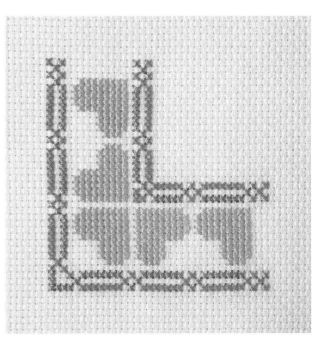

TIPS

● *Coton perle* is slightly more difficult to work than stranded cotton. If you use one length for too long it tends to lose its sheen and also to come unravelled, so cut short lengths, and give them the occasional twist to maintain their texture.

● When you are sticking down the embroidery over the frame, use a ruler or any straight edge to check that the lines of your Aida are straight. The straighter you can get them, the better your final frame will look.

● Don't cut out the inside from the embroidery until you have mounted it on the adhesive card-board; it is much easier to position it correctly while the centre is still intact.

■

VARIATION

■

You can use all kinds of different colour combinations to stitch your photograph frame, but do keep the colours relatively light and pretty if it is for a wedding photo. The sample shown here is stitched to the same design as the main project, but is worked in two strands of stranded cotton, using light and dark pink with blue, on 14 hpi white Aida.

BLUEBIRD PICTURE

Easiness rating: fairly difficult
Time-to-stitch rating: long-term

The two bluebirds are the symbols of true lovers, taken from the Chinese story of the willow-pattern plate. If you don't know the story, the lovers turned into bluebirds to escape the wrath of a disapproving father. Have a look the next time you come across a willow-pattern plate, and you will see the bluebirds hovering over the bridge – another essential part of the story! This 'stained-glass' version is based on a stained-glass panel made for the Stoke Garden Festival in England several years ago. The two birds fit perfectly into a square design, their beaks just touching, and the Chinese feel is enhanced by the blue-and-white colour scheme and the oriental pattern of the border.

■
MATERIALS
■

- One piece of white Aida, 46 cm (18 in) square, 11 hpi
- Anchor stranded cotton in the following colours:
    403 black (three skeins)
    137 light blue (three skeins)
    139 mid-blue (four skeins)
    134 dark blue (four skeins)
- Medium tapestry needle
- Frame to fit the finished tapestry (mount cut to an aperture of 34 cm [13½ in] square)

■
PREPARATION
■

1 Press the piece of Aida with a warm steam iron.
2 Use lines of tacking or a fading pen to mark the centre lines of the design.

■
STITCHING
■

3 Beginning at the centre of the design (see the chart overleaf), use three strands of black cotton in your needle to stitch all the black outlines for the birds.
4 Stitch the eyes in black.
5 Using three strands of the light or mid-blue as appropriate, fill in the bird shapes inside the bodies and wings.
6 Using three strands of dark blue and beginning at one corner, stitch the border pattern.

■
FINISHING
■

7 Lay the embroidery face-down on a soft cloth and press on the reverse side with a warm steam iron. Straighten the grain of the fabric if necessary during pressing.
8 Stretch the embroidery across a piece of backing board or adhesive cardboard of the appropriate size for your frame.
9 Frame your picture as required. Here I have used two pieces of mounting board, one of which is white, cut to the very edges of the embroidery, and then surrounded by a frame of blue mounting board stuck on top.

A detail of this picture can be seen on page 39. It shows part of the border pattern and the black outline stitching around the central design.

137

139

134

403

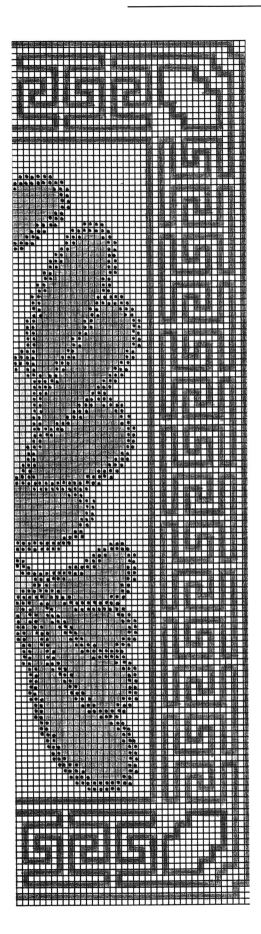

● If you stitch the black outlines of the birds first as suggested, all you then need to do with the blue threads on the birds is to fill in the outlined shapes, without having to count each line.

● If you would prefer a bit of extra definition on the eyes of the birds, work backstitch round each side of the black cross stitch, using one strand of the black cotton.

● When you begin to work the border, stitch a little of the inner single-stitch border first at the top-left or bottom-right corner, where it is easy to count it correctly. Then begin working the corner motif and the key pattern, and work the key pattern all the way round before completing the inner border.

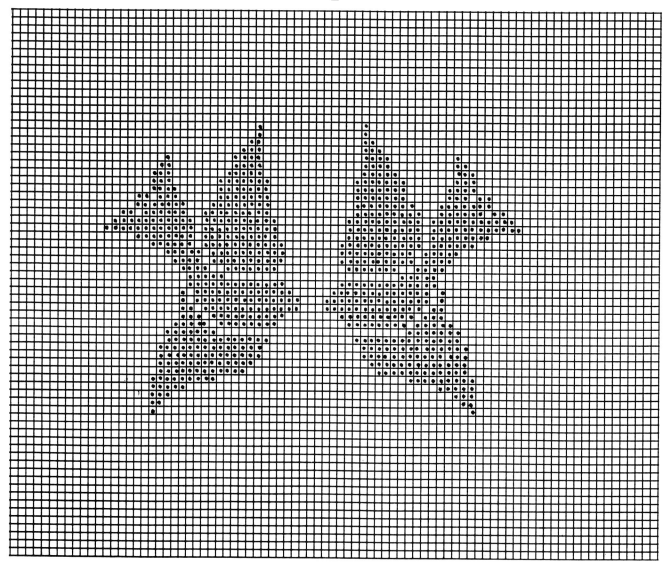

VARIATION

The quaint little picture opposite is less daunting to stitch than the large bluebird picture shown on page 37. It would make a perfect small present for a wedding or anniversary – or you could stitch it as a wedding card, perhaps as an accompaniment to the larger picture!

Here the design shown on the small chart has been stitched as *petit point* (miniature cross stitch) in ordinary royal blue sewing thread, although you could use one strand of stranded cotton or silk just as effectively. The fabric is 22 hpi white Aida, but the design would look equally good on white or pale blue evenweave linen. A border of diamonds or hearts could be added to complete the design (see the charts on pages 30 and 34). The finished picture has been mounted in a miniature blue frame which sets it off perfectly.

A pretty blue frame complements this miniature cross stitch (petit point) bluebird design which is taken from the Chinese story of the willow-pattern plate.

ANNIVERSARIES

HEART PICTURE

Easiness rating: medium
Time-to-stitch rating: medium

Hearts are always good symbols for anniversaries, and this picture features a heart motif at the centre of a series of exotic borders.

The inspiration for this ornate picture came from illuminated manuscripts, and the gold thread and jewel-like colours also reflect the richness of the medieval age. The gold mount and the gold border of the dark-wood frame add still more rich decoration to the panel.

The flowered border and the central initials incorporate tiny gold beads. It is easy to build these into your cross stitches by working the underneath stitch first, then bringing your needle up to do the top stitch; thread a bead on to your needle at this stage, and the top stitch of the cross holds it in position.

I have used the initials P and S inside the heart, but of course you can use any initials that are appropriate. Choose from the alphabet on pages 50–1, then simply leave the appropriate spaces inside the heart when you come to step **5**.

■
MATERIALS
■

- One piece of cream Aida, 22 cm (9 in) square, 11 hpi
- Anchor stranded cotton, one skein each in the following colours:
    - 047 red
    - 134 blue
    - 188 green
    - 119 purple
- One spool of Madeira gold thread No. 40, shade Gold 6
- Pack of small gold beads
- Medium tapestry needle
- Gold mounting board
- Frame to fit the finished embroidery

■
PREPARATION
■

1 Press the piece of Aida with a warm steam iron.
2 Mark the centre of the design with tacking stitches or a fading pen.
3 Choose the initials that you wish to use on the panel and mark them in on the chart in a contrasting colour in place of the P and S.

■
STITCHING
■

4 Beginning at the centre of the design and working outward (see the chart overleaf), stitch all the squares marked with a dot in gold thread, using three strands of the thread in your needle. This thread, like most metallics, tends to catch on itself and on other things, so make sure that each stitch lies properly flat before you go on to the next one.
5 Using three strands of cotton in your needle, fill in the inside of the heart with red. Leave the blocked-in squares blank for the moment.
6 Using three strands of cotton, fill in the area outside the heart and the narrow border outside the flowered border with purple.
7 Using three strands of cotton, fill in the narrow inner border and the outside border with green.
8 Using three strands of cotton, fill in all the unmarked squares of the flowered border with blue.
9 Now is the time to add the beads. Using three strands of gold thread, stitch the lower stitch of each cross in the ordinary way. When your needle emerges for the top stitch, thread a gold bead over the needle and complete the cross stitch; your bead should sit in the centre of your stitch. Work the centres of the flowers, and the initials in the middle of the heart, with beads in this way.

The rich colours of medieval illuminated manuscripts have been used as inspiration for this ornate anniversary panel. Tiny gold beads adorn the central heart motif and the pretty flower border.

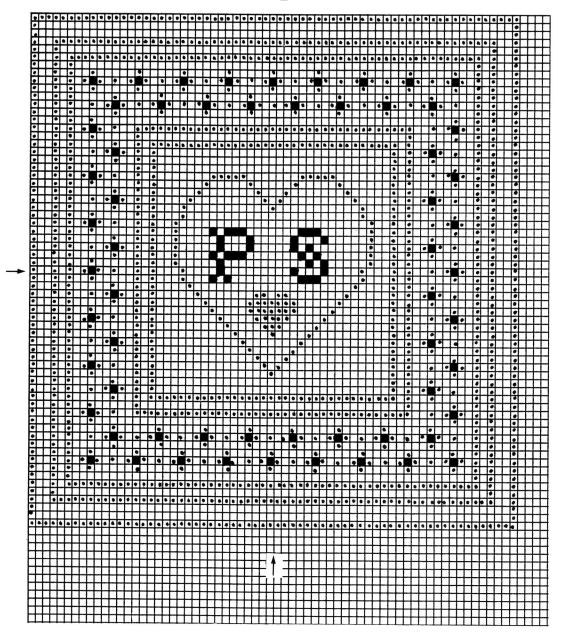

FINISHING

10 Lay the embroidery face-down on a soft cloth and press on the reverse side with a warm steam iron.

11 Cut a piece of gold mounting board to fit your frame, and then cut a central area out of the mount to measure 14·5 cm ($5\frac{3}{4}$ in) square.

12 Stretch the embroidery centrally over the backing board of your frame. Place the backing board and the mount together and check that the aperture in the mount and the position of the embroidery coincide exactly.

13 Assemble the frame.

VARIATION

For the simple card shown here, I have taken the central heart and initials from the main chart and stitched them on to a piece of 11 hpi white Aida in purple and mauve. The Aida was then mounted in a heart-shaped card blank and padded with a heart-shaped piece of thin wadding before the final gluing, to give it a slightly three-dimensional texture.

The colours in the main heart panel on page 45 can be varied by stitching the motif in different colours. If you do not want to use bright colours, softer shades can be used, such as pink, blue and yellow – or stitch your picture in just one colour and gold.

ANNIVERSARY SAMPLER

Easiness rating: medium
Time-to-stitch rating: medium

The tree of life is another motif found in many traditional pieces of cross-stitch embroidery, and it seemed an appropriate motif for this anniversary sampler. The alphabet is also a traditional one; variations of this letterform have been discovered in hundreds of samplers in Britain and North America, and it is still an attractive and legible choice. Work out the names you intend to put into the sampler, and incorporate them in the spaces marked on the chart (see overleaf).

The traditional feel of this design is enhanced by the delicate green-and-pink colourway, picked out with tiny squares of creamy yellow and worked on a cream background. The cream mount and walnut frame add to the old-fashioned aura.

MATERIALS

- One piece of cream Aida, 23 × 46 cm (9 × 18 in), 11 hpi
- Anchor stranded cotton, one skein each (unless specified otherwise) in the following colours:
    - 211 dark green
    - 208 mid-green (two skeins)
    - 206 light green
    - 075 pink
    - 301 yellow
- Medium tapestry needle
- Frame to fit the finished tapestry

PREPARATION

1 Press the piece of Aida with a warm steam iron.
2 Mark the centre of the fabric with tacking threads or a fading pen.
3 Decide on the names that you wish to include and draw them up on graph paper, using the alphabet from the sampler and spacing the lettering so that it looks even.
4 Mark the central line of each name.

STITCHING

5 Beginning in the centre of the fabric and working from the centre of the chart outward, stitch in the alphabet using three strands of mid-green cotton.
6 Using three strands of cotton throughout, stitch in the trees and the top row of leaves and flowers in the colours indicated.
7 Starting at the central vertical line and working outward, follow the charts you have drawn up to stitch in the two names, using three strands of pink cotton.
8 Finally, stitch in the bottom row of leaves and flowers, checking carefully that they match up with the top row.

FINISHING

9 Remove any tacking threads. Lay the embroidery face-down on a soft cloth and press on the reverse side with a warm steam iron. Straighten the grain of the fabric if necessary during the pressing.
10 Stretch the embroidery across the backing board of the frame, or stick it down over adhesive cardboard cut to the correct size.
11 Using cream paper or mounting card, cut a mount to the correct size for the frame.
12 Cut a rectangular aperture in the mount so that it will fit close to the edges of the embroidery (put the mount and the embroidery together, lining up the edges, to check that they fit exactly).
13 Assemble the frame.

The sampler on the opposite page has been designed using a traditional alphabet theme, with a tree of life motif stitched on each side of the letters. The tree is repeated, using different colours, in the little card below the sampler.

VARIATION

This little card has been made using some of the elements from the main sampler chart. For a totally different look, I have worked the design in shades of blue and pink on a background of white linen (25/26 hpi) with a silver thread running through it. First I stitched a tree motif with three shades of blue instead of the three shades of green on the chart, using three strands of stranded cotton across three threads of the linen. I then stitched in the blossoms on the tree in three strands of pink, and used the same pink to stitch in two initials taken from the alphabet on the sampler.

You could use this colour scheme to stitch the whole of the sampler chart if you prefer. This design would also lend itself well to the one-colour treatment shown in the table-mat on page 103.

208   075   206   301   211

TIPS

● When you are stitching the alphabet, keep checking the alignment of the letters and rows against each other so that you know you are keeping exactly to the chart.

● When you are drawing up your names, you won't necessarily want to space the letters so that there are the same number of squares between each pair. It is more important to space them *visually*, so that there don't seem to be any gaps and no two letters look too close together.

CELTIC LOVE-KNOT PICTURE

Easiness rating: medium
Time-to-stitch rating: medium

This design is actually a quilting pattern known as True Lovers' Knot, which seems a perfect motif for an anniversary picture. Here I have translated the smooth lines of quilting into a line of cross stitch, which changes colour through a delicate mixture of pinks, blues and purples as it weaves over and under itself in true Celtic style. Although the design looks quite complicated, it is actually quite easy and fairly quick to stitch.

This project uses the same traditional alphabet as the previous project; you could add your own names as appropriate, or leave the design as a square or circular picture.

The blue mount is one which I bought ready-cut and which suited the embroidery very well. These specialized mounts can be hard to find, but if you can track down a good craft or needlecraft shop you will probably find that there are some in stock. Alternatively, you could take your picture to a picture framer, or refer to one of the many books available on this subject.

■ MATERIALS ■

● One piece of white Aida, 35 × 25 cm (13½ × 10 in), 11 hpi
● Anchor stranded cotton, one skein each in the following colours:
    144 light blue
    145 mid-blue
    146 dark blue
    108 light purple
    109 mid-purple
    111 dark purple
    073 light pink
    055 mid-pink
    057 dark pink
● Medium tapestry needle
● Matching mount and backing board, or frame to fit the finished embroidery
● Craft glue or a hot-glue gun

■ PREPARATION ■

1 Press the piece of Aida with a warm steam iron, straightening the grain if necessary as you press.
2 Mark the centre lines of the fabric with tacking stitches or a fading pen.
3 On graph paper, draw up charts for the names you wish to use, using the alphabet on pages 50–1 and spacing the letters so that they look even.
4 Mark the vertical centre lines of each name.

■ STITCHING ■

5 Beginning in the centre of the fabric and at the centre of the chart (see overleaf), and working outward, stitch the pattern on to the fabric. Use three strands of cotton in your needle throughout.
6 Beginning at the centre lines of your name charts and aligning them with the vertical line going down your fabric, stitch the names in above and below the Celtic-knot design in the colours indicated. There should be a gap of three blank squares between the outermost parts of the knot design and the top or bottom of the names.

■ FINISHING ■

7 Lay the design face-down on a soft cloth and press on the reverse side with a warm steam iron. Straighten the grain if necessary during pressing.
8 Stretch the embroidery across a piece of backing board or adhesive board cut to the same size as the mount or frame.
9 If you are using a mount, use craft glue or a hot-glue gun to stick the mount around the front of the embroidery, aligning the edges of the two rectangles carefully. If you are using a ready-made frame, assemble the frame.

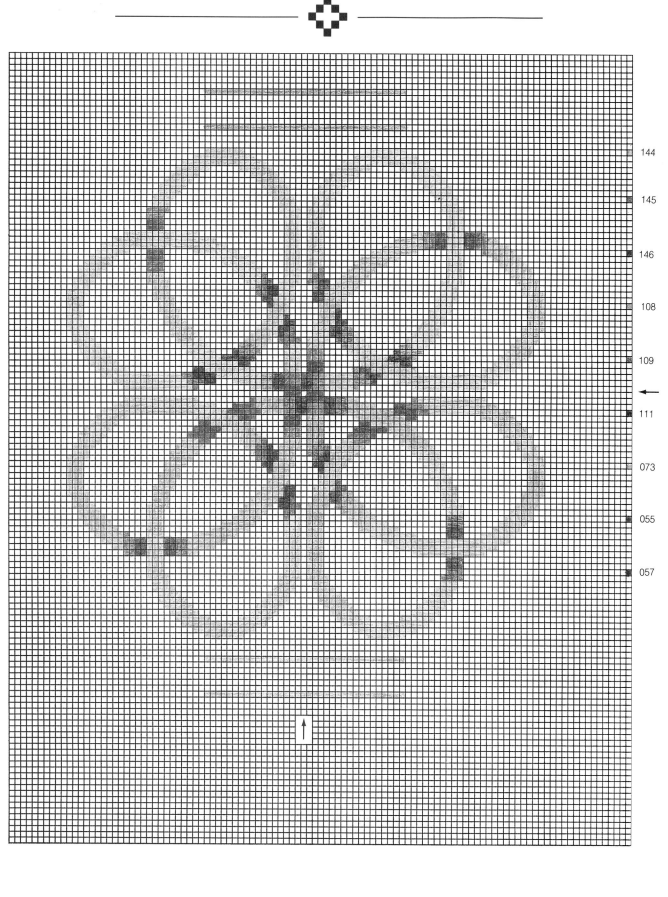

144

145

146

108

109

111

073

055

057

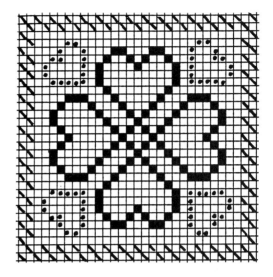

TIPS

● As you work this design, you will probably find that you are often turning the fabric round to make the stitching easier as you follow the curved line. If you do this, be very careful that your cross stitches all still have the top stitch going in the same direction.

● If your mount has decorative shapes cut out of it (as the one in the photograph does), make sure that your piece of Aida is large enough to go behind the holes if you have to trim it. Make sure too that glue doesn't squeeze out of the holes!

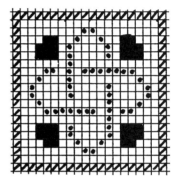

■

VARIATIONS

■

The two charts here show much simpler interlocking Celtic-knot designs, which would be just right for cards, pincushions or tiny embroidered keepsake pictures. The hearts incorporated into the designs make them especially suitable for anniversary, wedding or engagement presents. Work them in strong royal colours such as blues, jade greens, crimsons and purples, like the colours in the heart picture on page 45, or stitch them in soft pastels for a more gentle look.

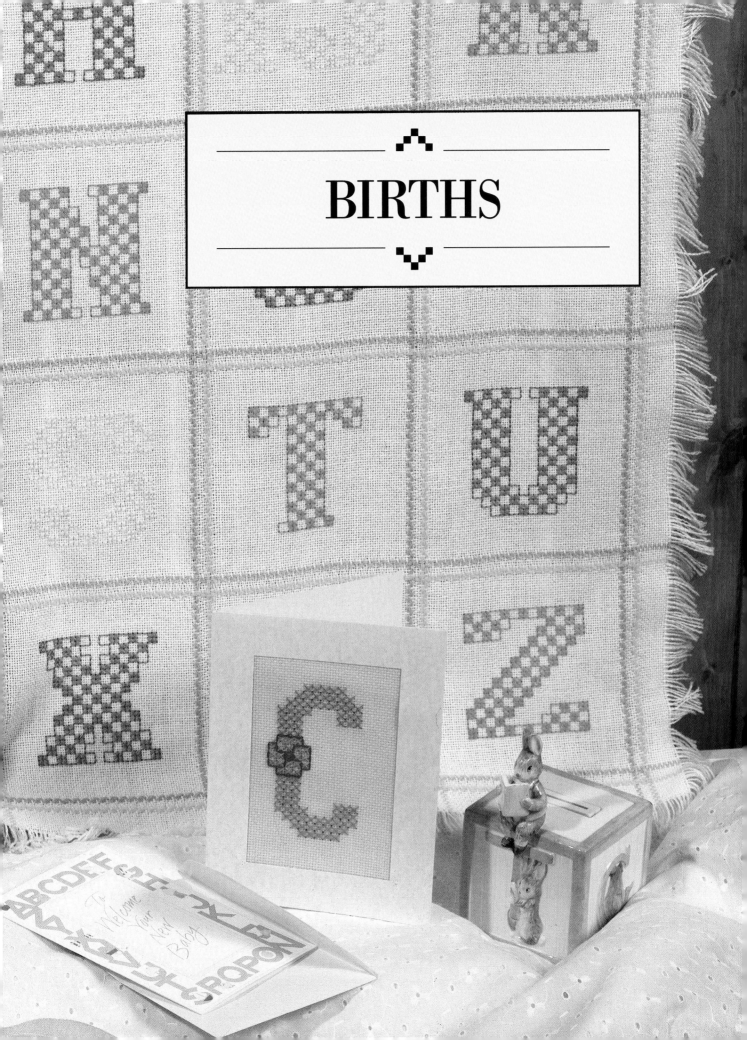

BIRTHS

INITIAL CARD

Easiness rating: very easy
Time-to-stitch rating: very quick

It is often difficult to know what to get for a new baby; many of the birth-congratulation cards in the shops are too 'cute', as are some of the presents. This congratulations card doubles as a small present, as it can easily be framed as a keepsake. If you are feeling ambitious, you could even stitch the new baby's whole name rather than just an initial, using the chart overleaf.

The card is very quick and easy to do. The very open cross stitch combined with backstitch gives the impression of blackwork, another counted-thread technique. The simple flower shape in the centre of the initial is made from a block of cross stitch; the impression of overlapping petals is produced by the different directions of the backstitches.

■ MATERIALS ■

- One piece of pale green Aida, 18×14 cm ($7\frac{1}{2} \times 5\frac{1}{2}$ in), 14 hpi
- Anchor stranded cotton, one skein each in the following colours:
    209 green
    055 pale pink
    059 dark pink
- Cream card blank with rectangular aperture $14 \cdot 5 \times 9 \cdot 5$ cm ($5\frac{3}{4} \times 3\frac{3}{4}$ in)
- Craft glue

■ PREPARATION ■

1 Press the piece of Aida with a warm steam iron, straightening the grain if necessary as you press.
2 Mark the centre of the fabric with tacking stitches or a fading pen.
3 Choose the initial that you will be using for the card, and work out its central point.

■ STITCHING ■

4 Use three strands of cotton in your needle. Working from the centre of the fabric and from the centre of the chart outward (see overleaf), stitch each cross stitch marked on the chart across three holes of the Aida. Use pale green cotton for the main letter, pale pink for the flower petals, and dark pink for the central stitch of the flower.
5 Using three strands of dark pink cotton, work backstitch around the flower petals as marked on the chart. Stitch each backstitch across three squares of the Aida.
6 Using three strands of green cotton, work backstitch in the same way around the edges of the letter.

■ FINISHING ■

7 Remove any tacking stitches. Lay the embroidery face-down on a soft cloth and press on the reverse side with a warm steam iron. Straighten the grain of the fabric if necessary during pressing.
8 Follow the instructions for the birthday card on page 14 for mounting the embroidery in the card frame and flattening the finished card.

TIPS
<ul><li>The stitches in this project are very long, so give your cotton an occasional twist as you stitch with it to stop the strands from splaying out.</li><li>When you are working such long stitches, it can be easy to pull them too tight and distort the fabric. Pull each thread through firmly but gently until it lies flat.</li></ul>

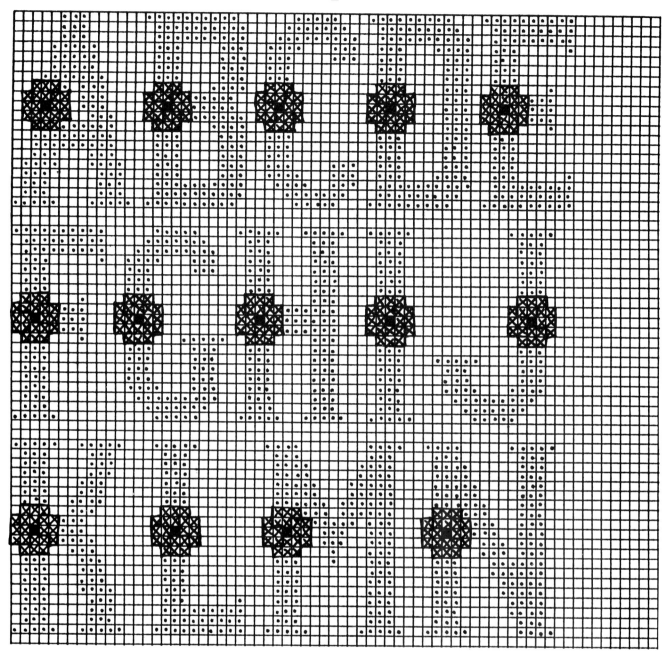

VARIATIONS

This design does not have to be confined to new babies; it would make an attractive keepsake for an older child's birthday too, or for an adult. Alter the colour scheme to suit your own preference or to tie in with a nursery colour scheme. A pink or blue initial with a yellow flower would look equally attractive, for instance, as would a yellow initial with a mauve flower. For a child you could stitch the design in bright primaries; for an adult you could use a much more sophisticated colour scheme such as olive green with golden orange, or tan and scarlet on a cream background.

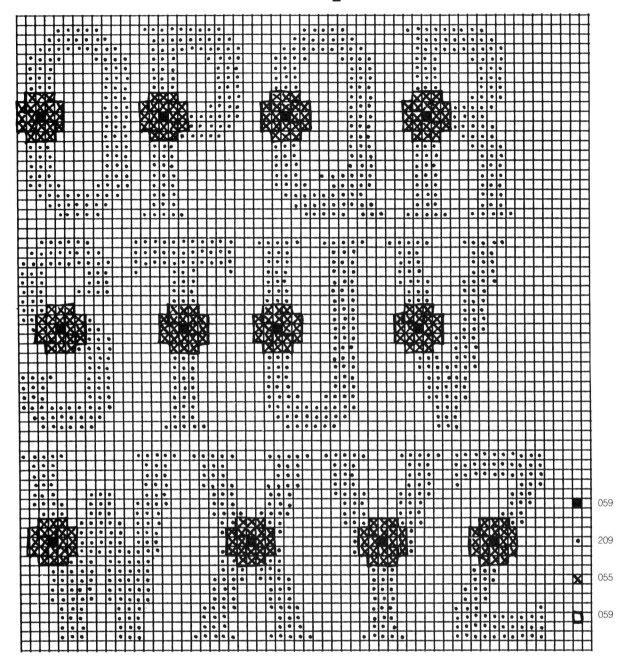

■	059
•	209
✕	055
⊔	059

NURSERY SAMPLER

Easiness rating: medium
Time-to-stitch rating: medium

Samplers used to be stitched by young children so that they could learn their alphabet while also learning a practical skill. Nowadays, many people enjoy stitching samplers *for* young children, and it is a lovely way to mark the birth of a new baby. This delicate sampler design is stitched in a range of eight mid-pastel colours, and the different colours used around the border are picked up in the lines of letters and numbers inside.

Although the border looks quite complex, it is actually very straightforward to stitch. It is built up from a simple repeat pattern of stripes which work their way through the eight colours in the same order each time. The four spare lines on the chart allow for three names and a date of birth, but the lines are fairly long, so if the recipient has four names you may be able to get two on a line. Work the names out on graph paper first so that you can make sure that they are centred beneath the alphabet and number lines.

MATERIALS

- One piece of white Aida, 41 × 36 cm (16 × 14 in), 11 hpi
- DMC stranded cotton, one skein each in the following colours:
  - 604 peachy pink
  - 959 turquoise
  - 209 mauve
  - 744 yellow
  - 764 blue
  - 3608 bright pink
  - 913 green
  - 352 orange
- Medium tapestry needle
- Frame to fit the finished tapestry

PREPARATION

1 Press the piece of Aida with a warm steam iron, straightening the grain if necessary.
2 Mark the centre lines on the fabric with tacking stitches or a fading pen.
3 On graph paper, work out the names and dates that you wish to include, using the alphabet and numbers on the chart overleaf as a guide. Use a separate line for each name if possible, and space the letters so that they look even.
4 Mark the vertical centre line of each name or date.

STITCHING

Use three strands of cotton throughout.
5 Beginning at the centre of your fabric and starting at the centre of the chart, work upward, stitching the numbers and the rows of the alphabet. Check that the lines are aligned correctly with each other by looking at the relationships of the characters at the ends of the rows.
6 Working downward from the centre of the design, stitch in the names and date, making sure that the centre line of your charted designs coincides with the vertical centre line marked on your fabric.
7 Following the chart carefully, count the squares on your fabric to find the lines marking the inner edges of the border. Mark these lines on each side of the design with a line of tacking stitches or a fading pen; this will help you to check exactly where the border should go.
8 Following the chart, stitch the border, using the same sequence of colours all the way round.

ABCDEFGHIJ
KLMNOPQR
STUVWXYZ
1234567890

JOSEPH
EDWARD
BARNARD
26.7.92

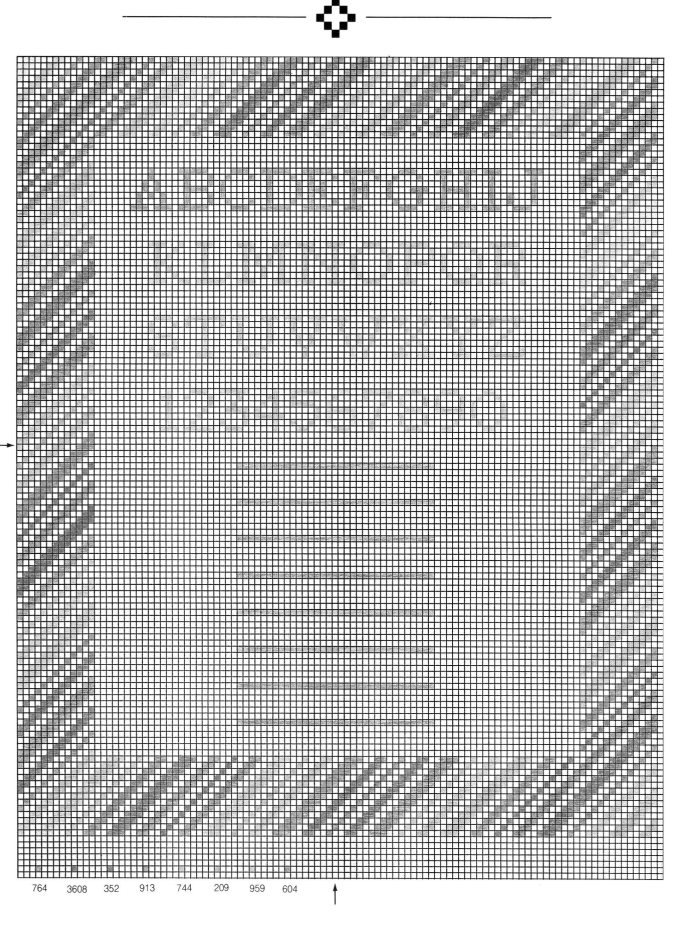

764   3608   352   913   744   209   959   604

FINISHING

9 Remove any tacking threads.

10 Lay the embroidery face-down on a soft cloth and press on the reverse side with a warm steam iron. As this design has a strong diagonal bias, you may find that your fabric has become slightly skewed, so straighten the grain as you press if necessary.

11 Stretch the sampler across the backing board of a frame or across a piece of adhesive cardboard.

12 Assemble the frame.

TIPS

● As this design uses the same sequence of colours all the way round the border, lay them out in front of you, in order, as you work. By doing this you will always have the next colour ready at hand.

● Because of the strong diagonals in this design, it is quite likely that your fabric will have pulled out of shape by the time you have finished stitching the border. If so, try to buy a piece of adhesive cardboard, or find a frame kit that contains a piece; this will help to keep the fabric in shape once you have straightened it. If you can't find adhesive cardboard, follow the instructions on page 11 for stretching the embroidery.

● The chart for this design mentions specific colours, but if you have similar colours in your workbox that need using up, you can easily substitute them. Just make sure that you have eight different colours of similar intensities, and that they look attractive together.

VARIATIONS

This design is given its soft nursery look by the gentle colours used, but there is no reason why you shouldn't work it in brighter colours for an older person. It would also adapt very well to a wedding sampler – you could put in something like:

> JOHN
> AND
> JANE
> DATE
>
> or
>
> JOHN
> MARRIED
> JANE
> DATE

As another way of using a similar border, the chart below shows a simplified version made into a design for a nameplate to go on a child's bedroom door. This chart uses three shades of blue, but you could work it in any colour combination. Simply extend the border as far as is necessary to fit around the name inside.

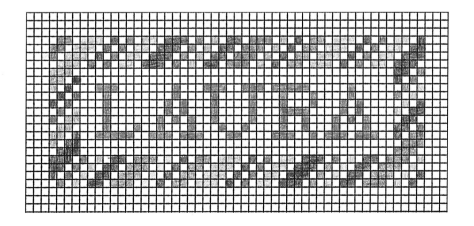

BABY BLANKET

Easiness rating: medium
Time-to-stitch rating: long-term

Delicate mid-pastels are used again in this attractive baby blanket, which can be used in an infant carrier, in a crib, as a playmat, or simply as an extra wrap on a chilly day. The colours of the cross stitch pick up the colours of the threads running across the blanket, and the finished item is washable, making it practical as well as pretty. As the blanket is divided into twenty-five squares and there are twenty-six letters in the alphabet, I and J are stitched in the same square, but as these are the narrowest letters anyway in a chunky alphabet it works out very well.

The cross stitches are given an unusual effect – almost like gingham – by working them in blocks of four and spacing them with even blocks of white. The backstitches around the letters define them and incorporate the white squares solidly into the design.

MATERIALS

- One Charles Craft Nursery-Time Afghan, 96·5 cm (38 in) square (*see also the Tips section on page 69*)
- DMC stranded cotton, five skeins each in the following colours:
    - 604 pink
    - 794 blue
    - 744 yellow
- Medium tapestry needle
- Tacking thread

PREPARATION

1 Press the blanket with a warm steam iron.
2 Count to find the centre of each row of squares, horizontally and vertically, and mark it with a row of tacking. Each square should be eighty or eighty-two threads wide, so your tacking lines should divide each square on the blanket into four smaller squares of forty or forty-one threads in each direction.
3 On your chart, mark in the centre lines of each letter horizontally and vertically with a faint coloured line, using the arrows as guidelines. This will help you to make sure that your letters are all aligned properly.

STITCHING

Use three strands of cotton in your needle throughout, both for the cross stitch and the backstitch.
4 Beginning at the centre of the top left-hand square, and working from the centre of the chart for the letter A outward, stitch the first letter in pink. For every X marked on the chart, stitch a block of four cross stitches, working each stitch across four threads of the blanket. For every dot marked on the chart, leave a white square the same size as a block of four cross stitches.
5 Outline the letter, as shown on the chart, using backstitch. Make each backstitch the length of one cross stitch, i.e., across four threads.
6 Go to the next square on the blanket and work the letter B in the same way, using blue thread instead of pink.
7 Work the letter C in the next square using yellow.
8 Continue to work your way along the rows of the blanket, following the same sequence of pink/blue/yellow, until you come to the ninth square.
9 For the ninth square, work your design out on graph paper so that you can fit both the I and the J into the square; the close-up detail on page 70 will help you to work out their relationship. Stitch this square, following your graph-paper chart.
10 Fill in the other squares in the normal way, keeping the colours in the same sequence.

Blocks of four cross stitches are built up into the letters of the alphabet to create an unusual gingham effect. Washable evenweave fabric can be used if you are unable to buy the type of blanket suggested opposite (see the 'Tips' section on page 69). Close-up details of three of the squares are shown on page 70.

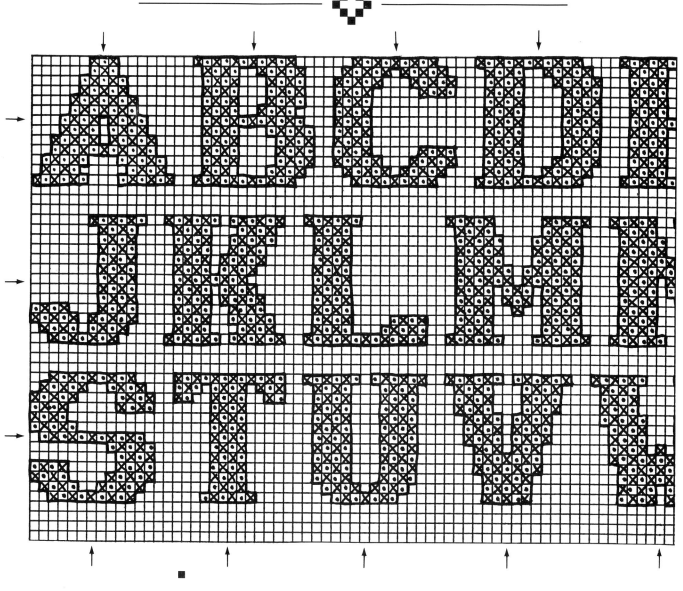

FINISHING

11 When your stitching is complete, remove all the tacking threads.

12 Lay the blanket face-down on a soft cloth and press on the reverse side with a warm steam iron.

13 Fringe the edges of the blanket to whatever depth you think looks best, pulling the threads out gently one by one so that the blanket doesn't pucker.

14 Run a row of straight or zigzag stitches in white along the inner edges of the fringe to prevent any more threads from coming loose.

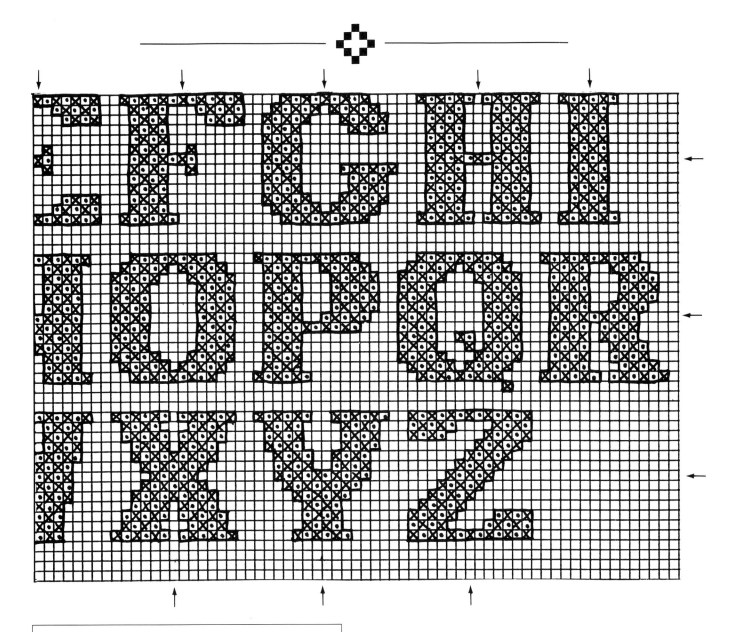

TIPS

● If you are unable to get the exact type of blanket suggested for the project, it is not difficult to make your own. Look out for a washable evenweave fabric (this one is a mix of trevira and viscose) with about fourteen threads to the inch, and divide it into twenty-five even squares of eighty threads using lines of coloured backstitch, whipped running stitch, chain stitch or something similar. Then just follow the instructions as above.

● When you are working the backstitch around each letter, make sure that you incorporate all the white squares as well (marked with a dot on the chart), as the backstitch does not always run directly around the cross-stitch blocks.

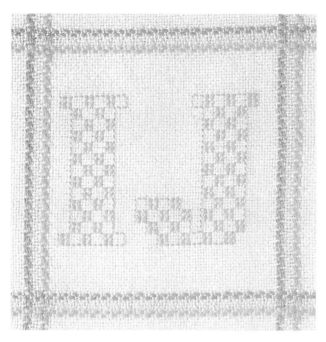

A close-up detail of the baby blanket on page 67. This shows how the letters I and J have been designed to fit into one square.

VARIATIONS

The photograph opposite shows one of the initials taken from the chart and worked as a tiny nursery plaque. It was stitched using three strands of stranded cotton on a scrap of 11-hpi Aida. The plaque has been finished off with a toning 10 cm (4 in) frame and a ready-made bow, but you could use the same idea for a simple card as well.

As you can see, you can make the letters more compact by working just one cross stitch, instead of a block of four, for each X marked on the chart, and leaving the same-sized square blank beside it; this idea could easily be adapted for a sampler of chunky checked letters.

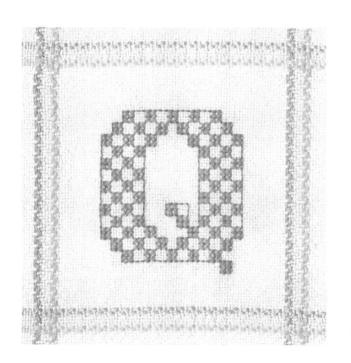

In these two details you can see how the stitching works, with blocks of four cross stitches together, and each stitch worked across four threads.

Opposite: This simple project in a single colour takes little time to make. The single letter could be enhanced by using metallic threads to highlight or outline the design.

EASTER

SPRING-FLOWERS PICTURE

Easiness rating: difficult
Time-to-stitch rating: long-term

This beautiful spring bouquet of daffodils, iris and forget-me-nots makes a spectacular picture. It is stitched on fine Aida to give a realistic appearance to the flowers and their shading. As you can see from the chart overleaf, you will need quite a number of colours to stitch the panel; you will also need quite a bit of patience, as everything is worked in two strands of cotton on 14-hpi fabric. Backstitch around the edges of the petals gives definition to each flower.

Although the chart is stitched as a picture here, it could also be worked as a central circle on a plain cushion-cover, or stitched much larger in tapestry wool or rug wool on coarse canvas to make a rug.

MATERIALS

- One piece of white Aida, 38 cm (15 in) square, 14 hpi
- Anchor stranded cotton, one skein each in the following colours:
    292 light soft yellow
    293 mid-soft yellow
    295 dark soft yellow
    302 light orange
    303 mid-orange
    304 dark orange
    109 light purple
    110 mid-purple
    102 dark purple
    097 light purple/pink
    099 mid-purple/pink
    101 dark purple/pink
    288 light bright yellow
    291 bright yellow
    050 light pink
    052 mid-pink
    175 light blue
    136 mid-blue
- Fine tapestry needle
- Frame to fit the finished picture, with a circular mount 28 cm (11 in) in diameter

PREPARATION

1 Press the fabric with a warm steam iron, straightening the grain if necessary.
2 Mark the centre lines of the fabric with tacking threads or a fading pen.

STITCHING

Use two strands of thread in your needle for all the cross stitches.

3 Beginning in the centre of the fabric and working from the centre of the chart outward, stitch the petals of the iris in the three shades of purple and the three shades of purple/pink.
4 Stitch the centres of the iris petals in the two shades of bright yellow.
5 Working from the centre of the chart outward, stitch the daffodils, using the three shades of soft yellow for the outside petals and light and mid-orange for the trumpets.
6 Using one strand of the dark purple, outline all the iris petals in backstitch.
7 Using one strand of the light orange, outline all the daffodil petals in backstitch.
8 Using one strand of the dark orange, outline the daffodil trumpets in backstitch.
9 Work the forget-me-not flowers in cross stitch in the two blues and pinks.

FINISHING

10 Lay the embroidery face-down on a soft cloth and press on the reverse side with a warm steam iron. Straighten the grain if necessary as you press.
11 Stretch the embroidery over a piece of adhesive cardboard or across the backing board of the frame.
12 Assemble the frame.

This lovely spring bouquet is stitched using two strands of cotton and the flowers are outlined in backstitch to add definition. A contrasting mount and frame complete the picture.

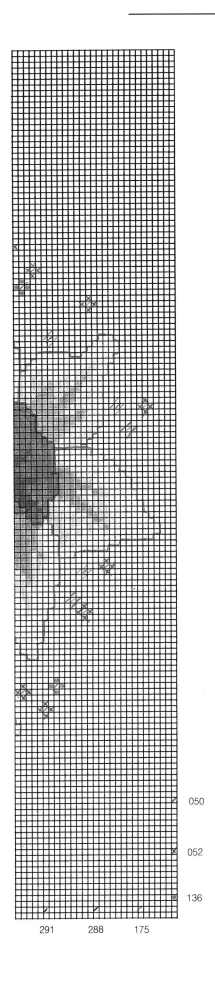

050

052

136

291   288   175

TIPS

- Try always to work in one direction across the canvas – for instance from top to bottom of the picture or across from left to right. This should help to ensure that you always keep the top stitches of the crosses in the same direction.
- When you are working the daffodils, complete each petal before you go on to the next. In the same way, complete each flower before you go on to the next; this will help you to keep an accurate count of your stitches across the wide chart.

VARIATIONS

The forget-me-nots on the picture make a pretty design themselves, so I have worked out a small wreath of flowers, shown opposite, which can be stitched in a fraction of the time that the large picture takes! Use the same shades of pink and blue as for the large picture, or use up toning skeins from your workbasket, for a dainty birthday card or a delicate design for a tablecloth or napkins. This design would work well stitched on the fabric you can buy in some craft shops especially for table linen; it is woven in a chequerboard pattern so that each alternate square is pierced for decoration in cross stitch.

A detail of the spring-flowers picture on page 75. The iris petals are stitched in three shades of purple and three shades of purple/pink. Two shades of bright yellow are used for the centres of the petals and flower. You can also see the little forget-me-nots clearly in this picture. Use the chart opposite to make a greetings card or a small plaque.

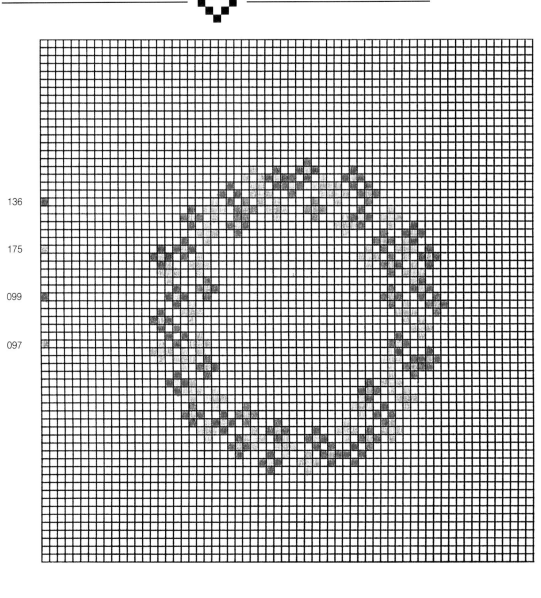

136

175

099

097

EASTER-EGG PICTURE

Easiness rating: medium
Time-to-stitch rating: medium

Everyone enjoys Easter eggs, and now here's your chance to create one that can be enjoyed all year round! This picture doesn't take too long to stitch, and will look pretty on the wall long after the Easter season is over and all the chocolate eggs have been consumed. The glittery gold bow makes an attractive contrast to the pastel colours and mid-shades of the egg, although if you prefer you could stitch the bow in two shades of yellow stranded cottons.

MATERIALS

- One piece of white Aida, 25 × 20 cm (10 × 8 in)
- Anchor stranded cotton, one skein each in the following colours:
  - 214 light green
  - 215 mid-green
  - 216 dark green
  - 218 very dark green
  - 073 light pink
  - 074 mid-pink
  - 076 dark pink
  - 888 brown
- Madeira metallic thread No. 40, one spool each of Gold 3 (light gold) and Gold 6 (dark gold)
- Fine tapestry needle
- Oval frame to fit the finished picture

PREPARATION

1 Press the fabric with a warm steam iron, straightening the grain if necessary.
2 Mark the centre lines of the fabric with tacking threads or a fading pen.

STITCHING

3 From the centre of the chart (see overleaf), count downward until you reach the edge of the bow. Beginning at the centre of your fabric, count the same number of squares downward and stitch the bow, using two strands of metallic thread in your needle.
4 Working outward from the bow and using one strand of stranded cotton, stitch in all the very dark green crazy-paving lines across the egg shape.
5 Using two strands of cotton, fill in all the coloured areas inside the dark green lines in the appropriate colours.
6 Using one strand of brown cotton, work backstitch along the edges and main lines of the bow as indicated on the chart.

FINISHING

7 Lay the embroidery face-down on a soft cloth and press on the reverse side with a warm steam iron. Straighten the grain of the fabric if necessary during pressing.
8 Remove the outer ring from the oval frame and lay the Aida across the inner ring. Make sure that the design is centred across the frame, and then replace the outer ring so that it traps the fabric between the two rings. Pull the fabric straight and taut.
9 Tuck the edges of the fabric out of sight on the back of the frame, trimming them down if this is necessary.

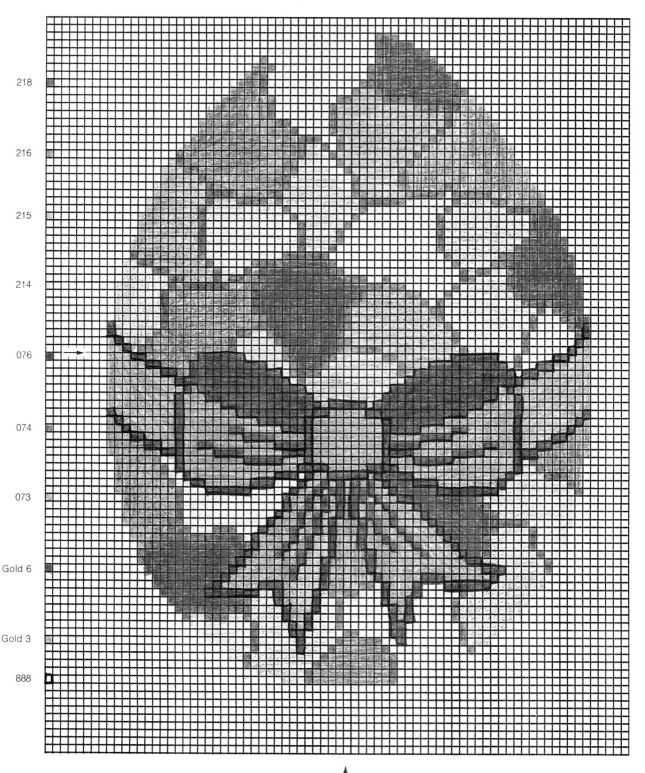

218
216
215
214
076
074
073
Gold 6
Gold 3
888

■

VARIATION

■

The photograph here shows a smaller Easter egg with a bow, stitched as a card. I have used two strands of Gutermann metallic threads throughout for the cross stitches, with the bow outlined in one strand of backstitch, all worked on a small piece of white 14-hpi Aida. The finished embroidery has been mounted on a textured silver card with an oval aperture measuring 7·75 × 5 cm (3 × 2 in), and softly padded with an oval of thin wadding beneath the embroidery to emphasize the rounded egg shape.

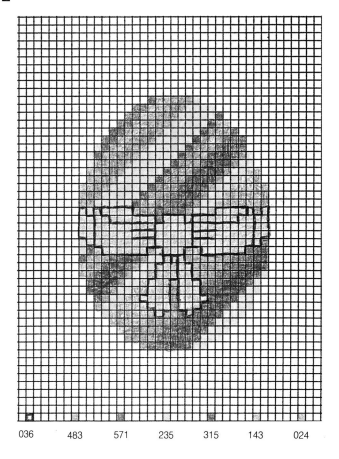

| 036 | 483 | 571 | 235 | 315 | 143 | 024 |

Metallic threads add a sparkle to this Easter-egg greetings card. A bow stitched in gold complements the glittering diagonal design and the oval shape of the egg is emphasized with a layer of thin wadding beneath the embroidery.

EASTER EGG-COSY

Easiness rating: easy to medium
Time-to-stitch rating: quick to medium

This cheerful Easter egg-cosy will make sure that your boiled egg doesn't get chilly on Easter Sunday morning – and, of course, you can use it the rest of the year round too! It doesn't take long to make, so you could stitch one as a present for each member of the family, perhaps working each in different colours so that there is no confusion over which belongs to whom. The front of the cosy is embroidered (and, of course, you can make a matching embroidered back if you feel ambitious), and it is then padded with wadding and lined. If you use washable wadding, it can even be laundered when it gets grubby.

MATERIALS

- One piece of white Aida, 18 cm (7 in) square, 11 hpi
- Anchor stranded cotton, one skein each in the following colours:
    142 blue
    293 pale yellow
    302 dark yellow
    111 purple
    063 dark pink
    085 pale pink
    187 pale aquamarine
- Medium tapestry needle
- Scraps of synthetic wadding
- Scraps of white cotton or polyester/cotton fabric
- White sewing cotton
- Small piece of white iron-on Vilene

PREPARATION

1 Press the piece of Aida with a warm steam iron, straightening the grain if necessary.
2 Mark the centre lines of the fabric with tacking threads or a fading pen.

STITCHING

Use three strands of thread throughout.
3 Starting at the centre of your fabric and beginning at the centre of the chart (see overleaf), work the row of blue stitching across the pattern, counting carefully.
4 Working outward on the chart and the fabric, stitch in the other rows of the design, completing each pattern before you move on to the next.

FINISHING

5 Lay the embroidery face-down on a soft cloth and press on the reverse side with a warm iron. Straighten the grain if necessary during pressing.
6 Cut a piece of Vilene to the same size as your square of Aida and iron it on to the back of the embroidery.
7 Trim round the edges of the embroidered shape to within 1·5 cm ($\frac{1}{2}$ in) of the stitching.
8 Press your white fabric.
9 Using the embroidered shape as a pattern guide, cut three shapes the same size from the white fabric.
10 Cut two pieces from the wadding the same shape, but 1·5 cm ($\frac{1}{2}$ in) shorter at the bottom.
11 Place the embroidered shape and one of the pieces of white fabric together, with the right sides facing, and tack and then stitch all the way round the curved edge, 1·5 cm ($\frac{1}{2}$ in) in from the edge.
12 Trim and clip the seam and turn the fabric right-side out.
13 Press with a warm steam iron on the plain side.
14 Place the other two pieces of white fabric right-sides together. Add one wadding shape on the top and one underneath, and tack all four layers together.
15 Stitch a seam through all four layers round the curved edge of the shapes.
16 Clip the wadding and the fabric to just outside the stitching line.

17 Slip the embroidered shape over the lining and wadding so that they fit comfortably together.

18 Turn under the raw edges at the bottom of the egg-cosy and slipstitch or overstitch the two layers together all the way round the hem.

This design would look just as effective in one or several shades of the same colour. Different motifs could be used and built up into patterns by referring to the charts at the end of the book.

142 293 302 111 063 085 187

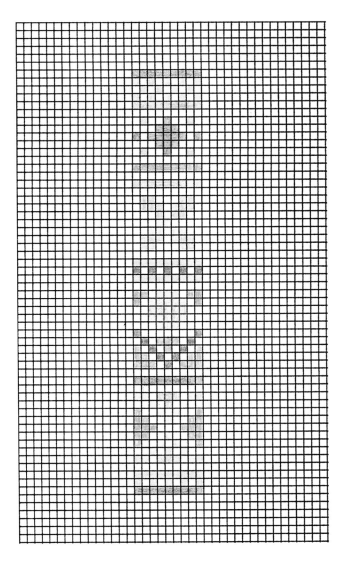

VARIATIONS

I have specified certain colours for stitching the egg-cosy, but this project can easily be worked from tail ends of embroidery skeins that you have in your workbox. The chart on this page shows another colour scheme that will give a different feel to the embroidery. It has the same sequence of patterned rows, but worked in a scheme of greens, yellows and turquoises. You could vary the colours infinitely; for a totally different look, try working the stitches on a coloured Aida background instead of white.

The patterned rows could be used as borders around a central motif, or they could be incorporated into sampler designs. Build up your own projects by referring to other ideas in this book.

CHRISTMAS

NATIVITY PICTURE

Easiness rating: fairly difficult
Time-to-stitch rating: medium to long-term

The nativity is the focus of Christmas, but it can be difficult to find attractive cribs and crib scenes. One answer is to create and stitch your own design; this starlit scene can become part of your annual decorating ritual. The figures are based on the bright, simplistic pottery nativity scenes made in South America, and the bold patterns of stripes and stars, and the stylized shapes, echo the folk crafts of that continent.

Mary, Joseph and the baby Jesus have all been given haloes which pick up the yellow and gold of the star. In ancient times, when most people were unable to read, religious pictures always followed certain conventions so that you could easily tell who was who. I have followed this convention in the design and given the Christ-child a halo with a cross pattern marked on it, while Mary wears the traditional blue robe.

MATERIALS

- One piece of white Aida, 50 × 30 cm (20 × 12 in), 11 hpi
- Anchor stranded cotton, one skein each (unless specified otherwise) in the following colours:
    - 403 black
    - 370 brown
    - 368 beige (two skeins)
    - 880 flesh
    - 293 mid-yellow (two skeins)
    - 047 red
    - 360 dark brown
    - 297 dark yellow
    - 240 pale green
    - 227 dark green
    - 060 light pink
    - 054 dark pink
    - 134 blue (two skeins)
- Gutermann metallic thread, one spool of 024 gold
- Medium tapestry needle
- Arched frame to fit the finished picture

PREPARATION

1 Press the Aida with a warm steam iron, straightening the grain if necessary.
2 Mark the centre lines of the fabric with tacking stitches or a fading pen.

STITCHING

Use three strands of cotton or metallic thread for all the cross stitches.
3 Starting at the centre of your fabric and at the centre of the chart (see overleaf), begin by stitching Joseph's hood and face.
4 Stitch Joseph's halo, using gold for the marked lines and the outline.
5 Stitch Mary's halo in the same way.
6 Stitch Mary's hood and face, and stitch the rest of her pink cloak edging.
7 Stitch the rest of Mary's cloak.
8 Stitch the rest of Joseph's cloak.
9 Stitch the manger, and baby Jesus's head and halo.
10 Stitch the star at the top of the picture.
11 Using one strand of black cotton, work backstitch around the manger, the haloes, and the main lines of Mary and Joseph as shown on the chart. Mary's mouth is made from three lines of backstitch.

FINISHING

12 Lay the embroidery face-down on a soft cloth and press with a warm steam iron. Straighten the grain of the fabric if necessary during pressing.
13 Trim the picture to size and stretch it over the backing board of the frame or over a piece of adhesive cardboard.
14 Assemble the frame.

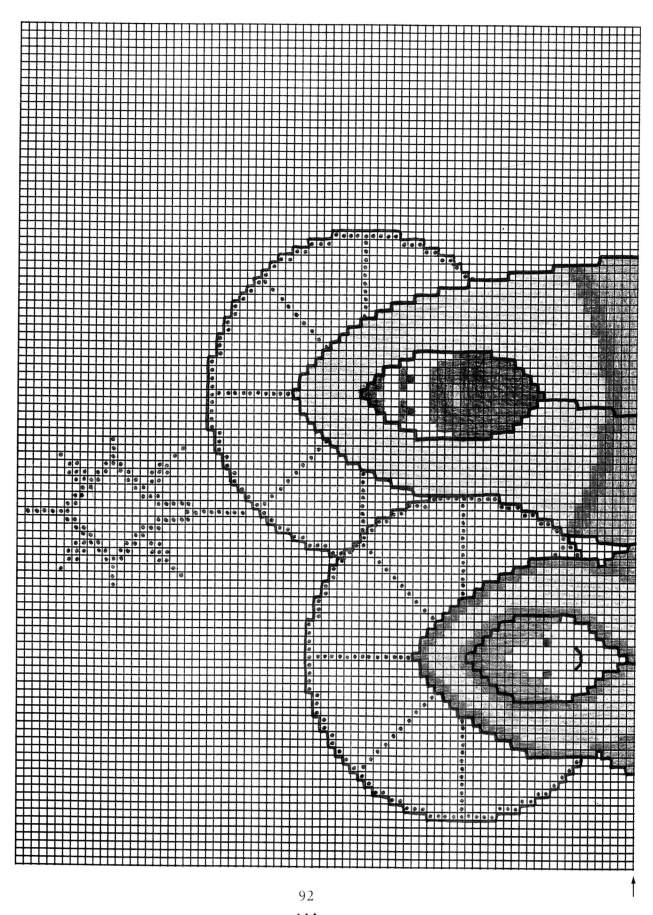

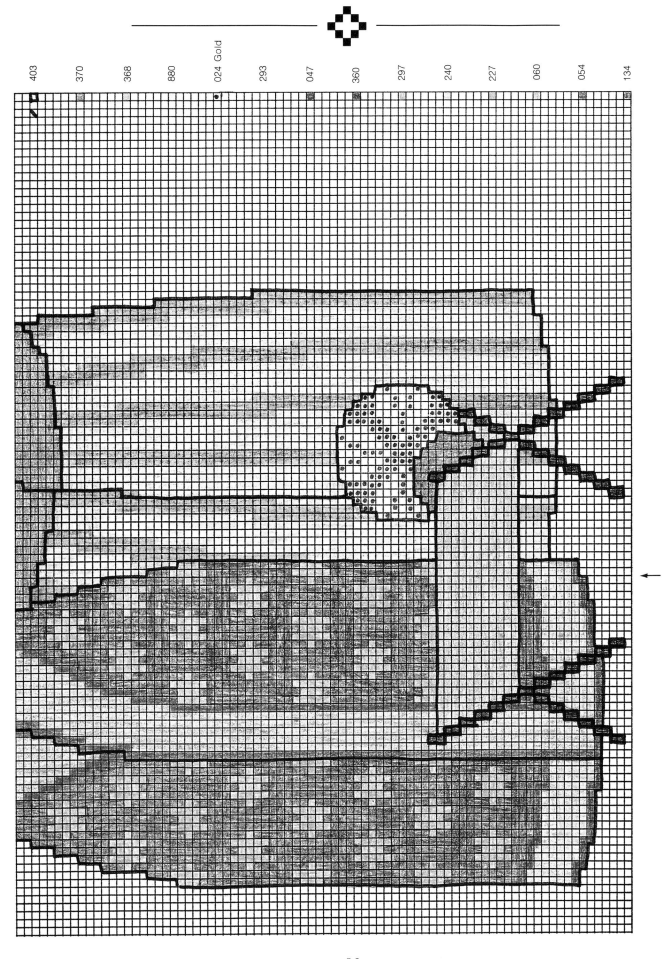

VARIATIONS

For an individual Christmas scene or card, you could stitch just one part of the nativity scene shown on the chart. The baby in the manger could be stitched with the star above him, or you could just stitch the star on its own as I have done for the example shown opposite. The shape of the star fits perfectly into the tiny Christmas-tree frame, making it into an unusual decoration for a tree or to hang from a mantelpiece or in a window.

A detail of the nativity scene on page 91. The baby and the manger could be stitched on to a small piece of white or coloured Aida and made into a special Christmas card for a friend or relative.

HOLLY WREATH

Easiness rating: fairly easy
Time-to-stitch rating: medium

Wreaths of holly, ivy, pine cones and ribbons are popular Christmas decorations, but they are not usually very durable. This attractive cross-stitch holly wreath can be used again and again; it doubles as a wall decoration, or as a centrepiece for a festive table setting.

The wreath is fairly big, but grows quickly because it is stitched with thick soft cottons across coarse Binca. Only two shades of green are used, but the leaves are made to stand out from each other with an edging of black backstitch, which also gives definition to the berries.

Once the embroidery is finished, the wreath is stitched into shape and given a soft padding of stuffing or wadding to make it three-dimensional.

MATERIALS

- One piece of pale green Binca, 50 cm (20 in) square, 6 hpi (*see also the Tips section on page 100*)
- Anchor soft cotton in the following colours:
  230 dark green (six skeins)
  205 light green (six skeins)
  046 red (three skeins)
  403 black (four skeins)
- Large tapestry needle
- Square of firm backing fabric, the same size as the Binca
- Wadding or stuffing
- Green sewing thread

PREPARATION

1 Press the Binca with a warm steam iron, straightening the grain if necessary.
2 Mark the centre lines on your fabric with tacking threads or a fading pen.

STITCHING

3 As there is no centre to this design, you need to begin at one edge. Start your stitching on one of the centre lines, matching it with one of the centre lines on the chart (see overleaf), about four holes in from the edge of your square.
4 Stitch the dark green squares first, all the way round the wreath.
5 Work round the wreath filling in the pale green squares.
6 Stitch all the red berries.
7 Using the black cotton, stitch round the edges of all the leaves and berries with backstitch, following the lines shown on the chart.

FINISHING

8 Lay the embroidery face-down on a soft cloth and press with a warm steam iron. Straighten the grain if necessary during pressing.
9 Press the piece of backing fabric.
10 Lay the backing fabric and embroidery together, right sides facing, and stitch round the outside of the wreath by machine. Stitch about 1·5 cm ($\frac{1}{2}$ in) outside the edge of the embroidery, and make smooth curves to follow the main lines of the leaves – don't try to follow the edges exactly, as they are squared and you want to smooth them out.
11 Trim the edges of the seams to within 75 mm ($\frac{1}{4}$ in) of the stitching; clip the curves with sharp scissors.
12 Carefully cut a hole in the centre of the embroidered fabric, about 5 cm (2 in) away from the embroidery, and turn the fabrics right-side out.
13 Press with a steam iron on the backing fabric.
14 By machine, stitch a line of straight stitch just inside the shaped edge to give it a crisp finish.
15 Slip small amounts of wadding or stuffing into the wreath shape between the two layers.

16 Using straight machine stitch, stitch a line of smooth curves, as before, about 1·5 cm ($\frac{1}{2}$ in) outside the embroidery on the inner edge of the wreath. Go over this line of stitching two or three times so that the edge doesn't fray as you turn it under.

17 Trim the excess Binca to 75 mm ($\frac{1}{4}$ in) beyond the stitched line.

18 Trim the backing fabric to the same shape as the Binca.

19 Turn under both raw edges so that the machine stitching is hidden, and pin them into place.

20 Tack the edges to hold them firm while you are stitching.

21 Stitch just inside the edges of the fabric with straight machine stitch, and then remove the tacking threads.

22 Fix a short loop of ribbon or cord to the back of the wreath so that you can hang it up.

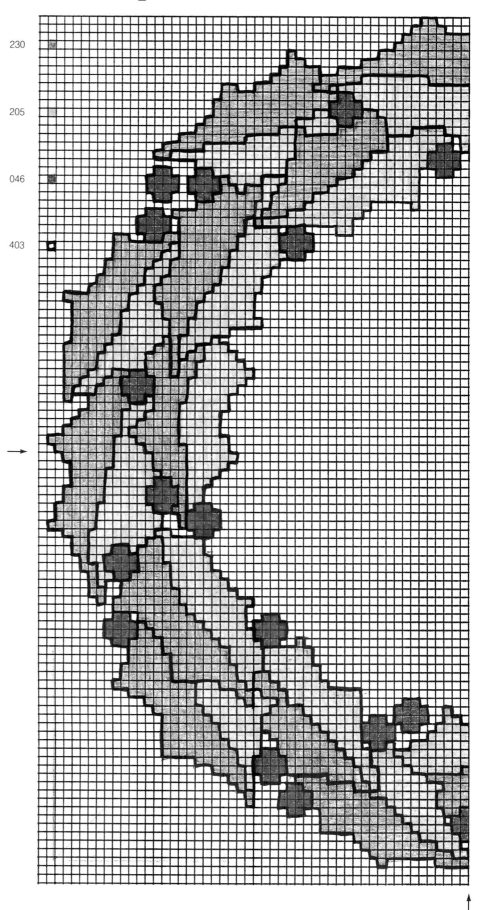

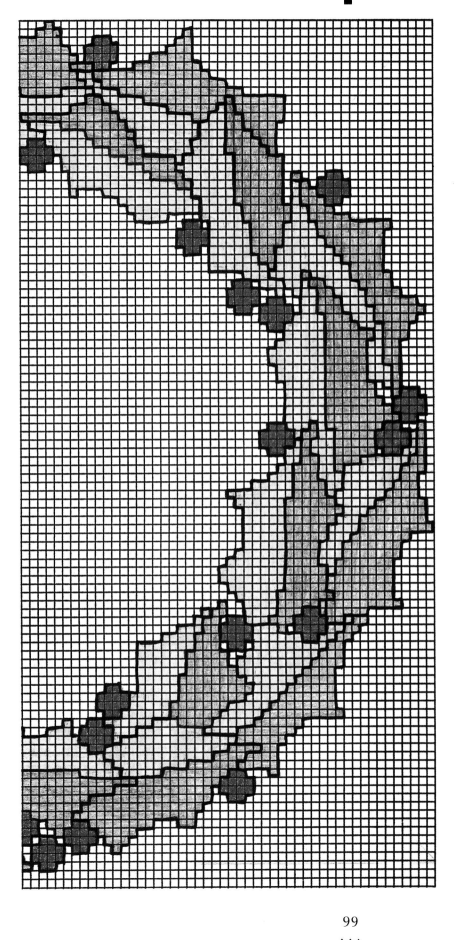

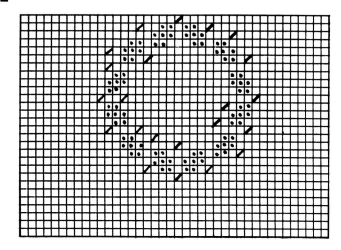

● Most Binca of this grade is sold in 50 cm (20 in) widths, so buy a 50 cm (20 in) length and you will have a square that is perfect for this wreath. Start your stitching about four squares in from one selvedge, on the centre line.

● When you are clipping the curved seams, use very sharp embroidery scissors with short blades so that you don't cut the stitching.

● Don't pad the wreath too much, or it will go out of shape and you won't be able to see all the stitching.

● As it is quite difficult to tell which way up the chart should be, mark your chart (if you are using a photocopy rather than the chart in the book itself) with TOP and BOTTOM, and mark your fabric in the same way with a water-soluble pen. By doing this you will always know that you are working the right section. Remove the marks from the fabric with a damp cloth when you have completed all the stitching.

VARIATIONS

Wreaths make pretty designs for smaller items as well; the chart shown above could be used for a card, a decoration for your Christmas tree, or a small plaque such as the one on the opposite page. Another nice idea would be to stitch several small wreaths across a set of table-mats or napkins for use on Christmas day.

Opposite: This simple design is built up using just dark green and red stranded cottons. Groups of cross stitches create the impression of holly leaves, with the red berries cleverly depicted by single stitches which are arranged around the central design.

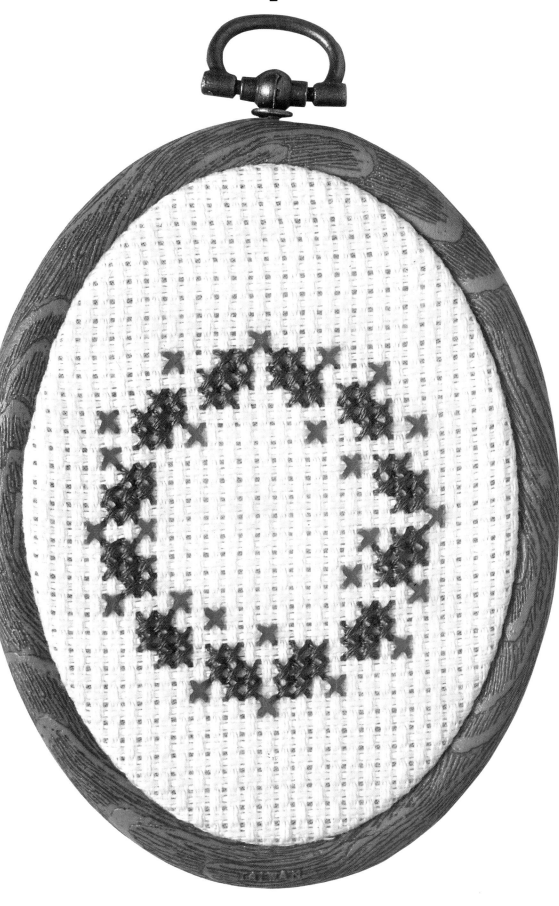

ANGEL TABLE-MAT

Easiness rating: medium
Time-to-stitch rating: long-term

The delicate one-colour embroidery on this Christmas table-mat is based on an art-nouveau design, originally used much smaller as a little decoration in a book. I have taken the design, enlarged it and simplified the lines, and translated it into a chart by tracing my version of the pattern on to squared paper. The single colour on midnight blue gives the impression of Victorian crochet lace – in fact, many crochet-lace patterns can be translated directly into cross stitch, as they are usually designed in squares!

This project takes some time to stitch, as the squares are tiny and there is a lot of counting, but the final effect is very attractive. Use the mat as a centrepiece for a candle or a simple Christmas decoration – nothing too fussy, so that you don't detract from the simplicity of the design itself.

■ MATERIALS ■

- One piece of navy blue Aida, 45 cm (17½ in) square, 14 hpi
- White stranded cotton (five skeins)
- Fine tapestry needle

■ PREPARATION ■

1 Press the Aida with a warm steam iron, straightening the grain if necessary.
2 Mark the centre lines of the fabric with tacking stitches or a fading pen.
3 As there is no stitching in the centre of the design, decide which edge of your Aida will be the bottom and measure in 2·5 cm (1 in) from the edge along the marked line. This will be where you begin your stitching.

■ STITCHING ■

4 Beginning at the bottom of the chart (see overleaf), and using two strands of thread throughout, start to stitch the design. Work up one side of the design from the centre bottom of the chart and complete one angel; work the wing after you have worked the body of the angel so that you know you have counted correctly.
5 Work your way up the other side of the chart to complete the second angel and its wing.

■ FINISHING ■

6 Remove any tacking threads.
7 Lay the embroidery face-down on a soft cloth and press on the reverse side with a warm steam iron. Straighten the grain if necessary during pressing.
8 Finish off the edges of the mat by turning them under and stitching a double hem, or by fringing them slightly. If you fringe the edges you may wish to stitch a row of straight stitches by machine where the fringing stops, so that you don't lose more threads than you want to. Alternatively, you could stitch on a piece of plain white or Christmas ribbon or braid to finish the edges, but, again, don't use anything too fussy or it will detract from the central design.

White worked on midnight blue is very attractive. Alternatively the angels could be stitched in different-coloured threads and the embroidery mounted and framed as a panel.

VARIATIONS

Blue makes an attractive background colour and gives a strong contrast, but you could also use Christmas green, scarlet, or even black to set off the design. If you don't want to stitch both angels, you could use just one at the edge of a large table-mat – or separate them, and stitch one at each end of a long table-runner for a Christmas buffet.

Other Christmas designs can look equally effective in the same colour scheme of white on a bright colour. In the example shown opposite, the small Christmas wreath from page 101 has been stitched in just three strands of white cotton on green Aida, and looks very pretty. Try adapting other designs which only use a few colours.

Opposite: a simple white cross-stitch design on green Aida. Very effective results can be achieved by using a single lighter colour on a dark background.

OTHER SPECIAL
OCCASIONS

CHINESE-STYLE INITIAL

Easiness rating: medium
Time-to-stitch rating: medium

This striking panel has been given an Oriental feel by the asymmetric outline of the letter, and the traditional Chinese clamshell design used round the border. The panel is multi-purpose, as you could put any initial in the centre – I have included outlines for every letter of the alphabet on pages 114–5. You could stitch the panel as a birthday or Christmas present, as a congratulations gift for a graduation, or just as an 'anytime' present. I have also included numerals along with the letters so that you could add dates (for a wedding or for a present to a new baby, for instance), or important numbers such as eighteen or twenty-five for a birthday or anniversary.

The panel is stitched in two shades of pink, plus tiny highlights in silver, and some lines of white-on-white outside the letter to add texture to the background. You will see from the chart that the white-on-white lines and the pink lines inside the letter form a regular grid across the square. If you alter the letter, simply work to the same grid but make sure that all the stitches inside the letter are pink and all those outside are white.

MATERIALS

- One piece of white Aida, 40 × 36 cm (16 × 14 in), 14 hpi
- DMC stranded cotton, one skein each in the following colours:
  915 dark pink
  603 light pink
  white
- Gutermann metallic thread, one spool of 041 silver
- Medium tapestry needle
- Frame to fit the finished panel

PREPARATION

1 Press the fabric with a warm steam iron, straightening the grain if necessary.
2 Mark the centre lines of the fabric with tacking threads or a fading pen.
3 Decide on the letter or letters you wish to use on your panel, and whether you wish to include any numbers. If you are using just one letter (or number), enlarge it so that it fits comfortably into the central square on the chart (see page 113). If you are using more than one letter or numeral, trace (or sketch freehand) your characters so that they fit into a square shape, and then enlarge or reduce them so that they fit into the central square of the chart.
4 Find the centre of your final design, and align it with the central point marked on your fabric. Trace the design on to your fabric using a fading pen.

STITCHING

Use three strands of stranded cotton or metallic thread throughout.
5 Using the dark pink thread, and following the design marked on your fabric, work cross stitches round the edges of the character(s). Follow the lines as closely as possible.
6 Check your traced central design against the chart on page 113, matching central lines, and count the squares to see where the nearest corner of the border should begin. Count very carefully, so that you can be sure that your design will be centred when the panel is complete.
7 Using dark pink thread, stitch the lines of cross stitch marking the inner edges of the border. Count the squares again carefully, working out from the centre lines.
8 Still using the dark pink thread, stitch in the clamshell outlines round the entire border, as marked on the chart.

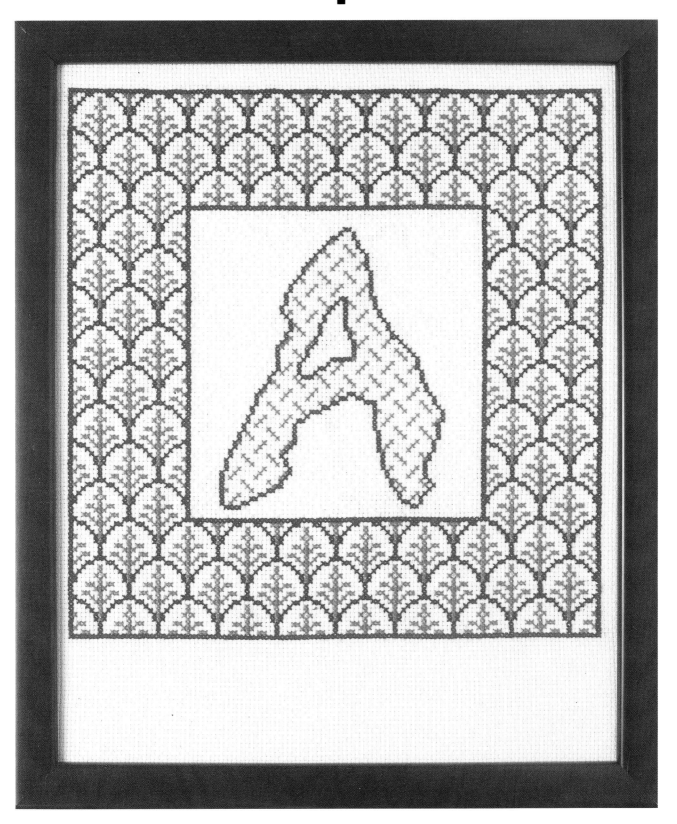

9 With dark pink thread, stitch in the outer edges of the border.

10 Using light pink thread, stitch in the floral design within each clamshell shape.

11 Using the metallic thread, stitch the highlighted square near the top of each floral motif.

12 Using white thread, begin at the top-right or top-left corner of the inner square and work the background grid of stitches around the whole area outside your character(s).

13 Using light pink thread, continue stitching the same pattern inside your character(s).

■

FINISHING

■

14 Remove any tacking threads. Lay the embroidery face-down and press on the reverse side with a warm steam iron. Straighten the grain if necessary during pressing.

15 Stretch the embroidery over the backing board of the frame or over adhesive cardboard, and trim to size.

16 Assemble the frame.

TIPS
● If you know that you are going to take quite a time to stitch your central design, mark it with a water-soluble pen instead of a fading pen. The marks made by the water-soluble pen will stay there as long as you want them. When you are ready to remove them, spray with water or sponge them away with a damp cloth, but make sure that you let the fabric dry completely before you iron it, or you will produce brown stains on the fabric. ● Work the whole of the dark pink clamshell outlines before you fill in any of the light pink floral motifs. It is much easier to see if you have made a mistake while you have the curved outlines of the design on their own. ● When you are stitching the grid pattern outside the character(s), you will see that it forms a very simple, regular, repeat pattern. Simply work your way round the white area, fitting in as many repeats or part-repeats as you can. Do the same thing inside the letters, continuing the pattern, but this time in pink. Remember that some of the squares of the repeat pattern may be taken up by the dark pink outline.

■

VARIATIONS

■

The alternative letters and numbers shown overleaf can be used for single or multiple designs within the patterned border, but you may like to vary the colour scheme as well. Two shades of blue or two shades of green look equally attractive, or you could mix gold and blue, green and mauve, yellow and orange, or red and silver. You could also try varying the colour of the background Aida.

As the design is square, it lends itself very well to cushion-covers. You could stitch two – one with each initial – for a wedding or anniversary present, or just make one for yourself with your own initial in the centre. The border looks attractive on its own, too; you could stitch it as a mirror-frame or photograph-frame, mounting it in the same way as the frame on page 33.

915   603   041   White
               silver

BCDE

FGHI

JKLM

NOPQ

RSTU
VWXY
Z1234
56789

MULTI-COLOURED ALPHABET

Easiness rating: medium
Time-to-stitch rating: long-term

I have included this project as another multi-purpose embroidery. It is ideal for a special occasion such as a graduation, or a thank-you present – times when a traditional sampler or a seasonal present are not quite right. Although the stitching is fairly straightforward, it is a surprisingly time-consuming undertaking, so start stitching in plenty of time for the special occasion. It is the kind of work to keep for cold winter evenings, when you can do a few letters at a time.

As you can see, the design is built up in reverse – rather than stitching the letters, you fill in the spaces in-between. This is the perfect project for using up all your spare skeins of embroidery cotton (perhaps the ones left over from other projects in this book, where you might have had to buy one skein of cotton and only used a little bit of it), so I have deliberately not given a colour key on the chart. I have stitched the alphabet in mid-bright shades, with a patch of a darker version of the same colour in each section to provide a bit of texture.

■
MATERIALS
■

- One piece of white Aida, 55 × 44 cm (21 × 17 in), 11 hpi
- Stranded cotton in assorted colours; you will need 12–15 full or nearly full skeins to complete the project, plus darker versions of the same colours if you wish to use them
- Medium tapestry needle
- Mounting board or frame to fit the finished project

■
PREPARATION
■

1 Press the fabric with a warm steam iron, straightening the grain if necessary.
2 Mark the centre lines of the fabric with tacking threads or a fading pen.

■
STITCHING
■

Use three strands of cotton throughout.
3 Working outward from the centre of the chart (see overleaf) and the centre of the fabric, stitch in the areas marked using the mid-shades of cotton. Use the matching darker shades to fill in smaller sections within each area of embroidery if you wish.

■
FINISHING
■

4 Remove any tacking threads.
5 Lay the embroidery face-down on a soft cloth and press on the reverse side with a warm steam iron. Straighten the grain of the fabric if necessary during pressing.
6 Stretch the embroidery across the backing board of the frame, or over adhesive cardboard, and trim to size.
7 Assemble the frame.

The letters are not stitched in this design. They are built up in reverse, with the background worked in multi-coloured cross stitch. This is an ideal project for using up left-over skeins of embroidery cotton.

TIPS

- If you are using lots of different colours, vary them as you work so that you do not have the same or similar colours near each other, and so that each colour is well-distributed across the embroidery.
- The finished embroidery is too large for most ready-made frames, so if you are making it full-size you will need to have a frame made specially. An alternative is to use mounting board in a toning colour, as I have done. The finished embroidery perfectly fitted a standard-sized piece of mounting board measuring 81 × 53 cm (32 × 21 in) when cut in half, with an aperture cut to 46 × 34 cm (18 × 13½ in).

VARIATIONS

You don't have to use lots of different colours to stitch the design. It would look equally effective in one, or several, shades of the same colour – you could choose a colour to tie in with a particular décor. If you prefer to stitch each area plain, without the darker section, that would look fine too.

If you are just looking for one unusual letter, you could take a single one from the chart and work it into a card or a plaque. In the example opposite, the letter A has been stitched in cream on to red Aida; instead of stitching round the outside of the letter, as in the alphabet, I have stitched in the shape of the letter itself. You can work single initials in this way, or combine letters from the chart that are not near each other in the alphabet, making them overlap as they do on the main alphabet panel.

A detail of the multi-coloured alphabet, showing the reversed-out design of the lettering. Opposite, the letterform is worked in cross stitch on a coloured background.

CHARTS FOR YOUR OWN DESIGNS

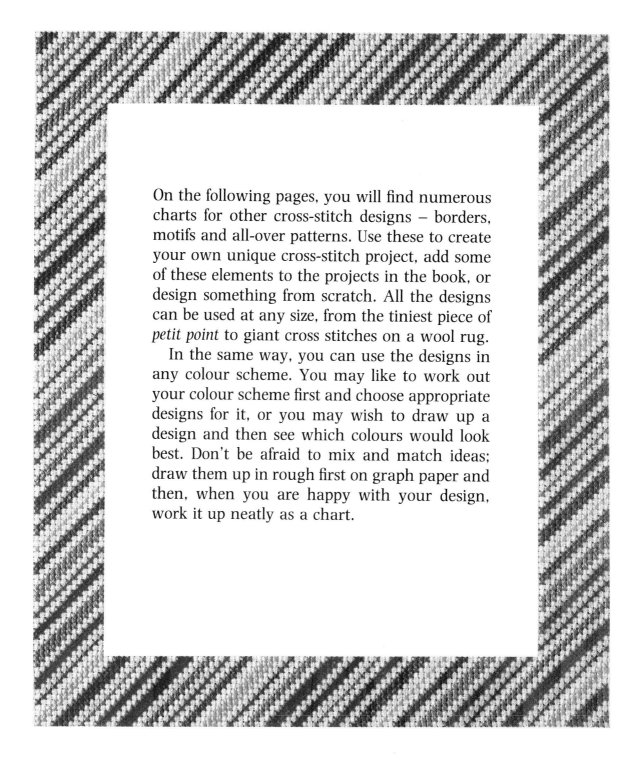

On the following pages, you will find numerous charts for other cross-stitch designs – borders, motifs and all-over patterns. Use these to create your own unique cross-stitch project, add some of these elements to the projects in the book, or design something from scratch. All the designs can be used at any size, from the tiniest piece of *petit point* to giant cross stitches on a wool rug.

In the same way, you can use the designs in any colour scheme. You may like to work out your colour scheme first and choose appropriate designs for it, or you may wish to draw up a design and then see which colours would look best. Don't be afraid to mix and match ideas; draw them up in rough first on graph paper and then, when you are happy with your design, work it up neatly as a chart.

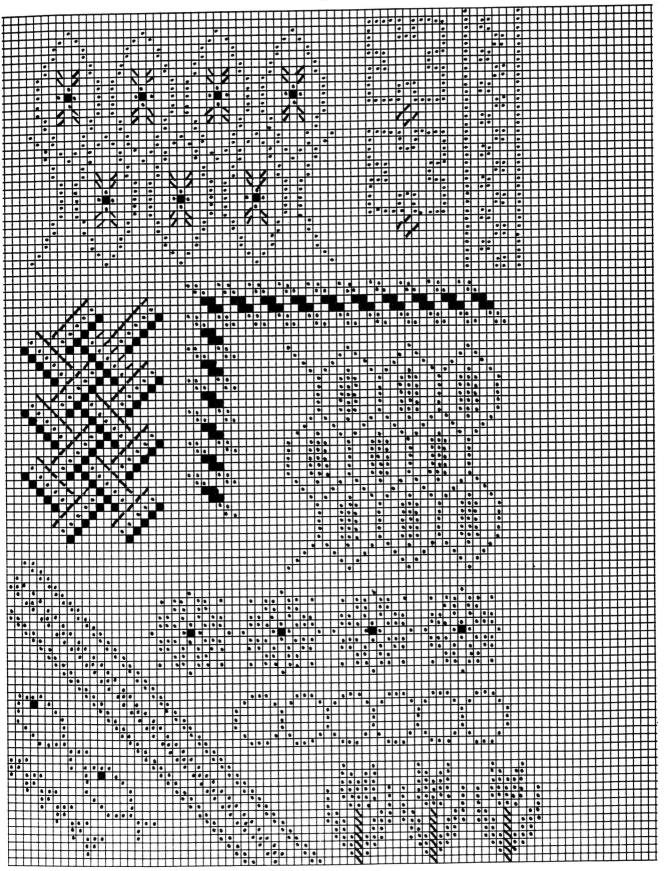

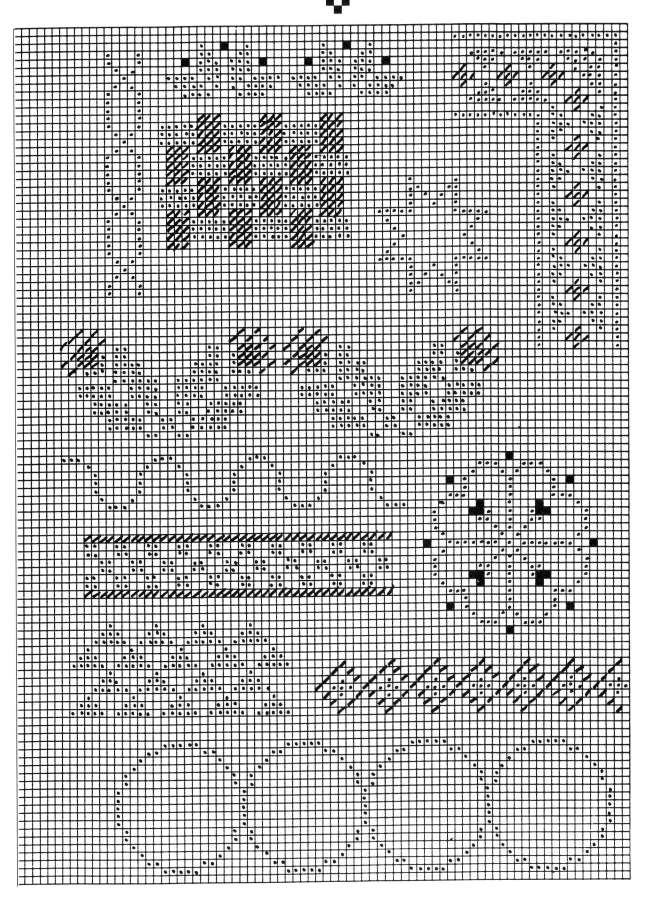

MANUFACTURERS AND SUPPLIERS

Most needlecraft and crafts shops, fabric and notions shops, the sewing and fabrics departments of large department stores, and needlecraft mail order houses stock the items used in this book. For information on retail sources in your area, contact the customer service departments of the following firms:

Thread and Floss
Gutermann of America, Inc.
P.O. Box 7387
Charlotte, North Carolina 28241–7387
in North Carolina: (704) 525–7068
all other locations: (800) 528–5187

Kreinik Manufacturing Company, Inc.
9199 Reistertown Road
Suite 209B
Owings Mills, Maryland 21117
(800) 537–2166

Madeira Marketing
600 East Ninth Street
Michigan City, Indiana 46360
(219) 873–1000

Susan Bates Anchor
Distributing by Coats & Clark, Inc.
Consumer Service Department
P.O. Box 27067
Greenville, South Carolina 29616
(803) 234–0331

Aidas, Linens, Damasks, and Other Prefinished Items
Charles Craft, Inc.
P.O. 1049
Laurinburg, North Carolina 28353
(919) 844–3521

Wichelt Imports, Inc.
Rural Route 1
Stoddard, Wisconsin 54658
(608) 788–4600

Zweigart Fabrics and Canvas
Weston Canal Plaza
2 Riverview Drive
Somerset, New Jersey 08873
(908) 271–1949

Glass Beads
Gay Bowles Sales, Inc.
P.O. Box 1060
Janesville, Wisconsin 53547
(608) 754–9212

Cardboard and Mounting Board
Crescent Cardboard
100 West Willow Road
Wheeling, Illinois 60090
(708) 537–3400

Framing Supplies
Nebletts Frames, Inc.
Route 7 – Box 260
Jackson, Mississippi 39209
(601) 922–6305

Sudberry House, Inc.
Colton Road – Box 895
Old Lyme, Connecticut 06371
(203) 739–6951

Mail Order
Clotilde, Inc.
1909 S.W. First Avenue
Fort Lauderdale, Florida 33315
(305) 761–8655

The Craft Gallery
P.O. Box 145
Swampscott, Massachusetts 01907
(508) 744–2334

G Street Fabrics
11854 Rockville Pike
Rockville, Maryland 20850
(800) 333–9191

Herrschners
Hoover Road
Stevens Point, Wisconsin 54492
(800) 441–0838

Rights Factory Outlet
Route 20
Sturbridge, Massachusetts 01566
(508) 347–2839